# MUSIC
## FOR THE
## VIOLIN AND VIOLA

# MUSIC
## FOR THE
# VIOLIN AND VIOLA

Compiled by

## HANS LETZ

*Volume II of the series*

*The Field of Music*

*edited by* Ernest Hutcheson, *President Emeritus*
*of the Juilliard School of Music*

# RINEHART & COMPANY, INC.
## NEW YORK · TORONTO

TO MY FRIEND ALBERT F. METZ

# PREFACE

During many years of teaching activity I have often felt the great need for a reference list which would offer a bird's-eye view of the violin and viola literature suitable for teaching and concert performance. While discussing my observations with a number of colleagues I found that many of them shared my views. We concluded that such a project would not only be of service to experienced pedagogues and performers refreshing their memories in regard to the available material in their field, but would also be musically helpful to students and young teachers. I decided to attempt the task of compiling a reference list fully realizing the great difficulty and responsibility involved.

I have chosen material from the best literature of the past and of today. For lack of space it was regrettably necessary to omit some works of importance and merit, and no attempt has been made to offer an exhaustive list of works for violin and viola.

The easy and elementary pieces are in most instances to be considered as study material. They may seem few in comparison with the total number of compositions, yet enough have been included to provide the needed foundation in technique and musicianship and to serve as stepping stones to the more mature repertoire. Under good instruction the student should not spend too much time on preparatory pieces; the sooner he can proceed to works suitable for actual performance the better.

The graded course of purely technical studies for violin has been selected to develop a balanced mastery of mechanical requirements. Naturally there are many other excellent methods and studies which would produce the same good results, and it is entirely within the teacher's choice to make whatever substitutions he thinks fit. Special methods for viola, too, may be added at will, though the fact that practically every viola student has studied the violin before taking up the viola suggests that he has gone through the fundamentals of a technique very similar in both instruments, and it is, therefore, quite feasible for him to start with the material in the list for advanced viola students.

From the many existing transcriptions and arrangements a limited but representative number have been chosen. In general preference has been given to original compositions.

The grading marks stress purely technical difficulties and indicate which positions are to be used. Of course it may easily happen that a piece is relatively simple technically while demanding advanced musicianship. But technical difficulty is fairly easy to define, whereas musical qualities are hard to indicate by grades. Full allowance must be made for this when consulting the grading signs.

In the "Remarks" referring to the small pieces and to pieces only of pedagogical value I have tried to point out their technical problems and general character. The annotations in connection with the more important compositions seem to me in many cases entirely inadequate, while the metronome marks indicate only approximate tempi. Words will never be sufficient to interpret the full meaning of music, which is elusive and intangible. It is much easier to express the meaning of words with music than to express the meaning of music with words. If the kind reader finds the "Remarks" in some ways interesting and stimulating I shall feel well rewarded for my efforts.

A word of thanks and appreciation is due to Mr. Charles R. Bietsch of G. Schirmer, Inc. for his tireless assistance in placing the necessary material at my disposal.

Hans Letz<br>
Hackensack, N.J.<br>
January, 1947

# MUSIC
## FOR THE
## VIOLIN AND VIOLA

## VIOLIN AND PIANO OR VIOLIN ALONE

| FIRST POSITION | FIRST, SECOND AND THIRD POSITIONS | HIGHER POSITION |
|---|---|---|
| A 1 Easy | B 1 Easy | C 1 Medium |
| A 2 Medium | B 2 Medium | C 2 Difficult |
| A 3 Difficult | B 3 Difficult | C 3 Very " |

| COMPOSER | TITLE, KEY & OP. | GR. | REMARKS |
|---|---|---|---|
| Accolay, J. B. | Concerto No. 1 in A Minor | C 2 | Strictly a student concerto Melodious and stimulating. |
| Achron, Joseph | Hebrew melody | C 3 | Sustained and poignant. Has also florid passages. |
| | Premiere suite en style ancien Op. 21 | | |
| | 1. Prelude | C 3 | Broad 16ths, detached bowing. |
| | 2. Gavotte | C 2 | Light and graceful bowing; some double stops. |
| | 3. Sicilienne | C 2 | Light and graceful in 6/8 rhythm. |
| | 4. Fughetta | C 3 | Spiccato and ricochet bowing. |
| | 5. Gigue | C 3 | Featuring trills and flying staccato. |
| Alard, Jean D. | Il Trovatore, Fantasie, Op. 37 | C 2 | Cadenzas, broad sostenutos, pointed rhythms, florid 16th passages. Only study material, not for concert. |
| | Faust, Concert Fantasia, Op. 47 | C 2 | Cadenzas, flying staccatos, ricochet bowing, double stops, florid 16th passages. Only for students. |
| Albeniz, Isaac | El Puerto, from "Iberia" (Heifetz) | C 2 | For concert use. Featuring ricochet and spiccato; has a Spanish flavor. |
| | Malagueña (Kreisler) | C 2 | For concert use. Featuring double stops and spiccato. |

| COMPOSER | TITLE, KEY & OP. | GR. | REMARKS |
|---|---|---|---|
| Albéniz, Isaac (Cont.) | Navarro (Heifetz) | C 2 | For concert use. Featuring singing tone, spiccato bowing, and octaves. |
| | Sevilla (Heifetz) | C 2 | For concert use. Charming and rhythmically interesting. |
| | Tango (Kreisler) | C 2 | For concert use. Graceful; featuring double stops and flying staccato. |
| | Cadiz (Stoessel) | C 2 | For concert use. Singing, but also rhythmically interesting. |
| d'Ambrosio, Alfredo | Ariette, Op. 56 | C 1 | Student material. Singing and smooth. |
| | Romance, Op. 9 | C 2 | Student material. Featuring singing tone. |
| | Serenade, Op. 4 | C 2 | Possibly for concert use. Easy flowing; some use of pizzicato. |
| | Canzonetta, Op. 6 | B 3 | For concert use. Graceful and light; some double stops. |
| | Little Canzonetta Op. 28 | C 1 | For studio. A graceful piece; some double stops. |
| Auer, Leopold | Concert Transcriptions: | | |
| | Agité (Dont) | C 1 | Fast 16th passages; detached bowing. |
| | Andante Cantabile, from Tchaikovsky's string quartet, Op. 11 | C 1 | Singing and expressive; use of mute. |
| | Melody in F (Rubinstein) | C 1 | For students. Featuring singing tone. |
| | Caprice No. 24 (Paganini) | C 3 | See Paganini . |
| | Chorus of the Dervishes from Beethoven's Ruins of Athens | C 3 | Excellent study in triplets for left hand. Fingered octaves. |

| COMPOSER | TITLE, KEY & OP. | GR. | REMARKS |
|---|---|---|---|
| Auer, Leopold (Cont.) | Dreams (Wagner) | C 2 | For studio. Featuring sustained tone. |
| | Melodie (Tchaikovsky, Op. 42) | C 2 | For concert use. Romantic and singing. |
| | Turkish March (Scherzo), from Ruins of Athens by Beethoven | C 1 | For pupils. Study in crisp rhythm and double stops. |
| Bach, Johann Sebastian | Air on the G String | C 1 | For concert and studio. Featuring broad and sustained tone. |
| | Arioso (Sam Franko) | C 1 | For concert and studio. Featuring singing tone. |
| | Choral "Herzlich tut mich verlangen" (Spalding) | C 2 | For concert use and for development of bow dexterity. |
| | "Come, Saviour of the Gentiles," Organ choral-prelude (E. Schenkman) | C 2 | For concert use. Warm and sustained. |
| | "Komm süsser Tod" (L. Tertis) | C 1 | For concert use. Broad and sustained. |
| | Adagio from the Toccata in C Major for Organ (Siloti-Kochanski) | C 2 | At present out of print. |
| | Sarabande, from English Suite No. 3 (Heifetz) | C 2 | Sustained and singing. |
| | Sarabande, from English Suite No. 6 (Heifetz) | C 2 | Broad and sustained. |
| | Two Gavottes, Nos. 1 & 2, from English Suite No. 6 (Heifetz) | C 2 | For bow dexterity and rhythm. |
| | Prelude in E, from Solo Sonata No. 6 (Kreisler) | C 2 | See under Bach, Solo Sonata No. 6. |
| | Partita in E Minor (Kochanski-Siloti) | C 2 | Prelude, broad and eloquent; detached 16ths. |

| COMPOSER | TITLE, KEY & OP. | GR. | REMARKS |
|---|---|---|---|
| Bach, Johann Sebastian (Cont.) | Partita in E Minor (Kochanski-Siloti) | C 2 | Adagio ma non tanto, fervently expressive. |
| | | | Allemande, stately and dignified. |
| | Sonatas for piano and violin: | | |
| | No. 1 in B Minor (edited by Hughes & Kortschak | C 2 | Adagio ♩= 55-63, warm and affectionate. |
| | | | Allegro ♩ = 92-94, suggests poise and dignity. Passages easy flowing. |
| | | | Andante ♩= 66-69, easy flowing but warm and singing. |
| | | | Allegro ♩= 112, spirited and rhythmically bold. |
| | Sonata No. 2 in A | C 2 | Andante ♪= 88, lofty and dignified. |
| | | | Allegro assai ♩= 126, joyful, festive and spirited. |
| | | | Andante un poco ♪= 88, suggesting fervor and warmth. |
| | | | Presto ♩ = 112, joyful and spirited. |
| | Sonata No. 3 in E | C 2 | Adagio ♪= 66, eloquently expressive and lofty. |
| | | | Allegro ♩= 98-100, animated and spirited. |
| | | | Adagio ma non tanto ♩= 56, dignified and eloquent. |
| | | | Allegro ♩= 120, spirited and lively. |
| | Sonata No. 4 in C Minor | C 2 | Siciliano (Largo) ♪= 92, reposeful, gentle, and expressive, with an easy sway. |

**Bach, John Sebastian (Cont.)** — Sonata No. 4 in C Minor — C 2

Allegro ♩ = 98-100, spirited and lively.

Adagio ♩ = 52, noble and eloquent.

Allegro ♩ = 104, animated and lively.

Sonata No. 5 in F Minor — C 2

Largo ♩ = 50, lofty and dignified.

Allegro ♩ = 108, rhythmically alive and animated.

Adagio ♪ = 60, violin chords sustained, piano part easy flowing.

Vivace ♪ = 63, lively and spirited.

Sonata No. 6 in G — C 2

Allegro ♩ = 110-112, festive, lively and happy.

Largo ♪ = 70, singing and expressive.

Allegro ♩ = 110, gay and lively.

Adagio ♪ = 58, singing with fervor and warmth.

Allegro ♩. = 84, gay and lively.

**Six Sonatas for violin alone:**

Sonata No. 1 in G Minor — C 3

Adagio ♪ = 46, noble and imaginative. In the character of an improvisation.

Fuga ♩ = 72, serious and authoritative.

Siciliano ♪ = 80, conveying a mood of pastoral peace and contentment.

Presto ♩. = 76, a movement of irresistible sweep.

| COMPOSER | TITLE, KEY & OP. | GR. | REMARKS |
|---|---|---|---|
| Bach, Johann Sebastian (Cont.) | Sonata No. 2 in B Minor | C 3 | Allemande ♪= 70,stately; at times warm and expressive. |
| | | | Double ♩= 84, playful and gamboling. |
| | | | Corrente ♩ = 144, vivacious and rhythmically decisive. |
| | | | Double (presto) ♩= 112, suggesting the gushing of a mountain torrent. |
| | | | Sarabande ♩ = 70, serious and stately. |
| | | | Double ♩ = 96, easy flowing. |
| | | | Bourrée ♩ = 76, crisp and rhythmical. |
| | | | Double ♩ = 96, playful and lively. |
| | Sonata No. 3 in A Minor | C 3 | Grave ♪= 50, like an improvisation of great nobility. |
| | | | Fuga ♩= 80, serious, severe and authoritative. |
| | | | Andante ♪= 58, expressing devotional fervor. |
| | | | Allegro ♩= 92, rollicking and brusque. |
| | Sonata No. 4 in D Minor | C 3 | Allemande ♩ = 72, dignified but not dragging. |
| | | | Corrente ♩ = 96, characterized by rhythmical sweep. |
| | | | Sarabande ♩ = 50, sustained and expressive. |
| | | | Giga ♩ = 76, demanding rhythmical directness and vigor. |

| COMPOSER | TITLE, KEY & OP. | GR. | REMARKS |
|---|---|---|---|
| Bach, Johann Sebastian (Cont.) | Sonata No. 4 in D Minor | C 3 | Ciacomna ♩= 52 to 62, based on a stately theme with variations of great imagination and contrast. |
| | Sonata No. 5 in C Major | C 3 | Adagio ♩ = 44, expressing greatness and nobility. |
| | | | Fuga ♩ = 70, suggesting dignity and authority. |
| | | | Largo ♪= 63, a most expressive movement of ethereal beauty. |
| | | | Allegro assai ♩ = 116, rhythmical, vigorous and alive. |
| | Sonata No. 6 in E Major | C 2 | Preludio ♩ = 116, full of life and vigor. |
| | | | Loure ♩ = 69, expressing heartfelt tenderness in innocent simplicity. |
| | | | Gavotte ♩= 80-84, suggesting rollicking humor. |
| | | | Menuetto I ♩ = 96-100, stately and dignified. |
| | | | Menuetto II ♩ = 96, tenderly expressive. |
| | | | Bourrée ♩ =96, robust and gay. |
| | | | Giga ♩ = 72, frolicsome and rhythmically decisive. |
| | Concerto No. 1 in A Minor (Spiering) | C 2 | Allegro (non tanto) ♩ = 92, rhythmically decisive; also affectionate. |
| | | | Andante ♪ = 60, affectionate and singing. |
| | | | Allegro assai ♩.= 112, driving ahead with dynamic buoyancy. There are also moments of tender lyricism. |

Bach, Johann Sebastian (Cont.) — Concerto No. 2 in E Major — C 2 — Allegro ♩ = 88, joyful, festive, and at times jubilant. The 16th passages are to flow melodiously. The double-stop section in the middle of the movement is witty and humorous. The allarganda builds up to a short but eloquent adagio phrase.

Adagio ♪ = 65. The opening tutti is dignified and eloquent; a movement of great emotional depth and fervor, serenity and nobility.

Allegro assai ♪ = 176. The opening idea is vigorous, followed by phrases of gracefulness, of persuasiveness, of rythmical vigor and of nimbleness. A movement of great vitality and contrast.

Concerto in D Minor for two violins — C 2 — Vivace ♩ = 88, serious and dignified; full of rythmical vitality.

Largo ma non tanto ♪ = 96, a duet of sublime beauty; a song of the angels.

Allegro ♩ = 92, vigorous and refreshing like mountain air; at times tender and affectionate.

Bax, Arnold — Mediterranean (Heifetz) — C 2 — A short and tangy piece.

Third Sonata — C 2 — I. Moderato ♩ = 132, affectionate and tender; at times dramatic and passionate.

II. Allegro molto ♩ = 138, restless, wild and rythmically virile. The lento expressive is tender and imaginative.

- 10 -

| COMPOSER | TITLE, KEY & OP. | GR. | REMARKS |
|---|---|---|---|
| Bazzini, Antonio | Allegro de Concert, Op. 15 (edited by Auer) | C 3 | For advanced students. Features every phase of violin technic. Brilliant and dashing. |
| | "La ronde des lutins," Scherzo fantastic | C 2 | A study in ricochet bowing; also an excellent concert piece. |
| Beethoven, Ludwig van | Menuet in G No, 2 | B 2 | A graceful and charming encore. |
| | (the same in a simplified edition by Ambrosio) | A 1 | |
| | Rondo in G (Burmester) | B 2 | For concert and studio. Varied graceful and light bowings. |
| | Turkish March (Scherzo), from Ruins of Athens (Auer) | C 2 | See under Auer. |
| | Romance in G, Op. 40 (Auer) | C 2 | Andante $\quad = 56$. The first theme in double-stops calls for a sustained cantabile. The middle section in E minor suggests a heroic character. |
| | Romance in F, Op. 50 | C 2 | Adagio cantabile $\quad = 58$. This romance also starts with a tender cantilene. The middle section in F minor suggests the outbreak of a sudden storm, but the piece ends on a note of peace and contentment. |
| | Sonatas for Piano and Violin: | | |
| | Sonata No. 1 in D, Op. 12, No. 1 | C 2 | Allegro con brio $\quad = 138$, grandiose sweep alternating with singing tenderness and whimsical playfulness. |
| | | | Andante con moto $\quad = 52$. Theme and Var. 1, friendly and warmhearted. Var. 2, playful. Var. 3, stern and (Cont.) |

| COMPOSER | TITLE, KEY & OP. | GR. | REMARKS |
|---|---|---|---|
| Beethoven, Ludwig van (Cont.) | Sonata No. 1 in D, Op. 12, No. 1 (Cont.) | C 2 | serious. Var. 4, sunny and amiable, changing to a mood of mystery but ending on a note of contentment. |
| | | | Rondo ♩.= 96, joyful and happy. |
| | Sonata No. 2 in A, Op. 12, No. 2 | C 2 | Allegro vivace ♩.= 104, light and sunny, playful and humorous. |
| | | | Andante più tosto, allegretto ♪ = 48, affectionate with a touch of sadness. |
| | | | Allegro piacevole ♩.= 84, happy and witty. |
| | Sonata No. 3 in E Flat, Op. 12, No. 3 | C 2 | Allegro con spirito ♩ = 126, royal and distinguished, at times humorous and playful. |
| | | | Adagio con molt'espressione ♪ = 66, noble and profound. |
| | | | Allegro molto ♩ = 126, jovial and exuberant, breathing a feeling of well-being. |
| | Sonata No. 4 in A Minor, Op. 23 | C 2 | Presto ♩.= 130, stormy passages of dashing virility alternating with phrases of caressing tenderness. |
| | | | Andante scherzosó, più allegretto ♪ = 84, whimsical and wistful; at times severe and serious. |
| | | | Allegro molto ♩ = 126, smooth and easy flowing, with a touch of wistfulness; in sharp contrast to two dramatic climaxes. |
| | Sonata No. 5 in F Major, Op. 24 (Spring Sonata) | C 2 | Allegro ♩ = 132, conveying a picture of spring in full bloom, breathing hope and confidence. |
| | | | Adagio molto espressive ♩ = 48, sublime, almost divine. |

| Beethoven, Ludwig van (Cont.) | Sonata No. 5 in F Major, Op. 24 (Spring Sonata) | C 2 | Scherzo, Allegro molto ♩. = 88, sparkling with wit and humor. |

Rondo (Allegro ma non troppo)♩ = 80-84, amiable and friendly, witty and playful; ending in intoxicating joy and happiness.

| | Sonata No. 6 in A Major Op. 30, No. 1 | C 2 | Allegro ♩= 120, friendly and sunny, playful and joyful. |

Adagio, molto espressivo ♪= 58-63, lofty, warm and affectionate.

Allegretto con variationi ♩ = 74, graceful and friendly. Var. 1, playful and fleeting. Var. 2, easy flowing and comfortable. Var. 3, brilliant and spirited. Var. 4, humorous and goodnatured. Var. 5 (Minore), serious and dignified. Var. 6 (Majore) Allegro ma non tanto ♩.= 98, easy flowing, happy and playful.

| | Sonata No. 7 in C Minor, Op. 30, No. 2 | C 2 | Allegro con brio ♩ = 144, a movement of great dramatic power; at times ominous and sinister, suddenly changing to a happier mood; then again playful and persuasive giving way to outcries of passion. |

Adagio cantabile ♩ = 54, a movement of great serenity and peace.

Scherzo (Allegro)♩ = 66-69, sparkling with wit and humor, at times giving way to brusque clownishness.

Finale (Allegro)♩ = 144, dynamic and powerful, sometimes witty, joyful and happy. The presto tempo is approximately ♩ = 160.

| COMPOSER | TITLE, KEY & OP. | GR. | REMARKS |
|---|---|---|---|
| Beethoven, Ludwig van (Cont.) | Sonata No. 8, Op. 30, No. 3 | C 2 | Allegro assai ♪.= 104, fleeting, dashing, friendly, sparkling, joyful and jovial. |
| | | | Tempo di menuetto ma molto moderato e grazioso ♩= 70, a movement of wistful tenderness and spiritual serenity. |
| | | | Allegro vivace ♩= 132, sparkling, playful and happy. |
| | Sonata No. 9 in A Major, Op. 47 (Kreutzer Sonata) | C 2 | Adagio sostenuto ♩= 40. Presto ♩= 150, dramatic and powerful, irresistible in its dramatic sweep. |
| | | | Andante con variazioni ♩ = 48,Theme and Var. 1, friendly and warmhearted. Var. 2, playful. Var. 3, striking a note of sad tenderness; almost imploring. Var. 4, amiable and sunny. |
| | | | Finale (Presto)♩.= 172, spirited, restless and elegant; at times powerful. |
| | Sonata No. 10 in G Major, Op. 96 (Spring Sonata) | C 2 | Allegro moderato ♩= 104. While the first movement of Sonata No. 5 portrays spring in full bloom, this movement conveys a picture of early spring. |
| | | | Adagio espressivo ♪= 48, one of Beethoven's most sublime adagios. In its spiritual devotion it is devoid of earthly desires. |
| | | | Scherzo allegro ♩.= 76, humorous and witty. The trio suggests an approaching village band, losing itself later on in the distance. |
| | | | Poco allegretto ♩= 102, jovial and happy, except for the profound and imaginative adagio. |

Beethoven, Ludwig van (Cont.) — Concerto in D Major, Op. 61 — C 3

Allegro ma non troppo ♩ = 112. Themes of loftiness and nobility; themes of manly strength, and themes expressing faith in God and man lend the background to this glorious movement. The beauties of a theme like the one in G minor of the middle section cannot be described by mere words. Heartfelt warmth without cheap sentimentality, freedom without license, imagination without exaggeration are the fundamental requirements for a satisfying performance. This applies to the entire concerto.

Larghetto ♩ = 48-52. The tutti of the orchestra states the first theme. It is repeated twice while the solo violin weaves figures of great imagination around it. After a sweeping crescendo, the orchestra tutti repeats it once more in full glory. A most poetic and free passage of the solo violin leads to a new theme in G major, one of the many sublime moments of the movement. We drift along in a dream-world until a crashing fortissimo brings us down to earth again.

(cadenzas by Joachim and Kreisler)

Rondo ♩.= 84, a joyful hunting theme of great rhythmical decision starts the movement. Two octaves higher it appears in a more delicate character. This happy mood continues up to the G minor theme. "Happiness through tears" may best express the character of (Cont.)

| COMPOSER | TITLE, KEY & OP. | GR. | REMARKS |
|----------|------------------|-----|---------|
| Beethoven, Ludwig van (Cont.) | Concerto in D Major Op. 61 (Cont.) | C 3 | this wistful section. An unexpected moment of indescrible charm occurs after the cadenza, when the first theme returns in A - flat major. Jubilation and joy bring this great concerto to a satisfying close. |
| Bennet, Robert Russel | Hexapoda, 5 studies in Jitter Opera | C 2 | A very colorful modern suite. |
| Bériot, Charles de | Airs Variés: No. 5 in E Major, Op. 7 | C 2 | Only for pupils. Developing all phases of violin |
| | No. 6 in A Major, Op. 12 | C 2 | playing. |
| | No. 7 in E Major, Op. 15 | C 2 | |
| | Scène de ballet, Op. 100 | C 2 | A charming stimulating piece for advanced students. Excellent for developing singing tone, bow control and lefthand technique. Very violinistic in every respect. |
| | Concerto No. 1 in D Major, Op. 16 | C 2 | The above remarks apply also to these five con- |
| | Concerto No. 2 in B Minor, Op. 32 | C 2 | certos. |
| | Concerto No. 6 in À Major, Op. 70 | C 2 | |
| | Concerto No. 7 in G Major, Op. 76 | C 2 | |
| | Concerto No. 9 in A Minor, Op. 104 | C 2 | |
| Berezovsky, Nicolai | Chant d'amour, Op.3 | C 2 | For concert and studio. Featuring singing tone. |
| | Gavotte | C 1 | For concert and studio. Featuring light staccato bowing. |
| Bloch, Ernest | Baal Shem (three pictures of chasidic life) 1. Vidui (contrition) 2. Nigun (improvisation) 3. Simchas Torah (rejoicing) | C 2 | These pictures are decidedly Hebrew in character. They are fine concert pieces; as teaching material they develop tone color and imagination. |

| COMPOSER | TITLE, KEY & OP. | GR. | REMARKS |
|---|---|---|---|
| Bloch, Ernest (Cont.) | Nuit exotique (Exotic Night) | C 2 | A colorful and imaginative piece; has a dramatic middle section. |
| | Mélodie | C 1 | Sustained and singing. |
| Boccherini, L. | Rondo (Willeke) | C 2 | Featuring flying staccato bowing. |
| | Minuet, from string quintet | B 2 | Quaint and charming. For studio and concert. |
| Bohm, Carl | Cavatina in D, Op. 314, No. 2 | B 2 | For studio only. Featuring singing tone. |
| | Moto Perpetuo, from the third suite | A 2 | For studio only. Featuring staccato bowing. |
| | Perpetual Motion, from "Little Suite" | A 2 | For studio only. Featuring very fast staccato. |
| | Introduction and Polonaise, from Arabesque No. 12 | B 2 | For studio only. A brilliant piece. |
| | Legend, Op. 314, No. 7 | C 1 | For studio only. Sustained and singing; has also double-stops. |
| Borowski, Felix | Adoration | C 1 | Is used in church and studio. Sustained and singing. |
| Brahms, Johannes | Contemplation (Heifetz) | C 1 | Singing and expressive. |
| | Cradle Song (Spalding) | C 1 | Calls for tenderness and simplicity; has some double-stops. |
| | Intermezzo in C Major, Op. 119, No. 3 (Spalding) | C 2 | Featuring double-stops. |
| | Waltz in A-flat (transcribed to A by Hochstein; simplified version by Ambrosio) | C 2 / A 1 | Poetic and affectionate. |
| | Waltz in E Minor, Op. 39 (Gordon) | C 2 | Sustained and expressive; some double-stops. |
| | Hungarian Dances (Transcribed by Joachim, two vols.), No. 1 in G Minor | C 2 | Allegro molto, warm and singing; middle section flippant; brilliant and fiery. |

| Brahms, Johannes (Cont.) | No. 2 in D Minor | C 2 | Allegro non assai, passionate and fiery; has also moments of melancholy. The vivo is happy and intensely rhythmical. |
| | No. 3 in F Major | C 2 | Allegretto, graceful. The "sotto voce" should create an effect of mysterious whispering. The vivace is joyful and enthusiastic. |
| | No. 4 in B Minor | C 2 | Moderato e sostenuto, languishing but warm. The vivace is fiery and wild with joy.<br><br>The molto moderato begins in a tantalizing whisper but builds up to fiery passion. |
| | No. 5 in G Minor | C 2 | Allegro, proud and passionate; at times light and sparkling; has also moments of melancholy. Vivace. The opening is exuberant and rhythmically decisive; then follows a pattern of two languishing ritardando measures being contrasted with two joyful and lively bars. |
| | No. 6 in B-flat Major | C 2 | Vivace, after the opening bar wistful and affectionate, contrasted with outbursts of wild joy. The molto sostenuto is proud and broad, almost pompous. The tempo primo takes on a little more motion. The "sempre vivace" drives relentlessly toward the end of the piece. |
| | No. 7 in A Major | C 2 | Allegretto. A tantalizingly hesitating rubato gradually gives way to outburst of joy and gracefulness. The sections after the second and third double bars strike a note of virility and rhythmical vigor. |

**Brahms, Johannes (Cont.)**

No. 8 in A Minor — C 2 — <u>Presto</u>. The first section is easy flowing with flautato bowing. It is repeated with an intensely warm tone an octave higher. Brilliant, sparkling and witty moments follow. The first idea returns but with all kinds of embellishments.

No. 9 in E Minor — C 2 — <u>Allegro non troppo</u>, rythmically clear-cut. <u>Meno mosso</u>, caressingly playful. <u>A tempo piu vivo</u>, proud and virile. The end of the piece "evaporates," so to speak.

No. 10 in G Major — C 2 — <u>Presto</u>, fiery and spirited, also playful. <u>Meno mosso</u>, stately. The passages in 16ths are to be dainty and sparkling.

Sonata No. 1 in G Major, Op. 78 — C 2 — <u>Vivace ma non troppo</u> ♩. = 52. After an opening of reverent tenderness, the syncopation passages culminate in an enthusiastic forte. The <u>con anima</u> is warmhearted, becoming even passionate and dramatic. The <u>grazioso teneramente</u> is intimate and graceful, losing itself by way of the calando in the clouds. The <u>più sostenuto</u> strikes a note of virile strength. A joyful and enthusiastic coda brings the movement to an end.

<u>Adagio</u>, ♪ = 56. The opening is warm and full, the violin entrance tenderly expressive. The <u>più andante</u> ♪ = 72 suggests a funeral march; but only for a short while. A heroic section follows. The piano part leads through ascending chords into a mood of mystery. The full-blooded and rich first theme comes back (Cont.)

- 19 -

Brahms, Johannes (Cont.) — Sonata No. 1 in G Major, Op. 78 (Cont.) — C 2 — in the tempo primo. The movement ends in the mood of a poetic farewell.

Allegro molto moderato ♩ = 88. The opening is tender and affectionate, almost imploring. The movement throughout has the character of great sensitiveness. In the E-flat major section, after the double bar, the second movement is called back to our mind, only to give way to a passage of exuberant joy. A sublime coda brings the sonata to a satisfying close.

Sonata No. 2 in A Major, Op. 100 — C 2 — Allegro amabile ♩ = 112. The opening conveys a feeling of well-being and friendliness. This feeling soon changes to a decisive rhythm and joy. A lyric section of great tenderness follows only to give way to ideas of virility and strength. Thoughts of an intimate character lead back to a repetition of the first parts of the movement. A section of 24 bars starts in a serious and philosophical mood and changes to mystery and transfiguration. The vivace indicates passion and joy, but soon the idea of the first theme returns in a dreamy and reposeful mood. A jubilant coda brings the movement to a joyful end.

Andante tranquillo ♪ =60, a movement of pastoral serenity and friendliness. The vivace ♩ = 168 suggests lightfooted gracefulness.

Allegretto grazioso ♩ = 66. The opening is warm and eloquent. The first pp. brings a mood of ghostly mystery but is contrasted
(Cont.)

- 20 -

| COMPOSER | TITLE, KEY & OP. | GR. | REMARKS |
|---|---|---|---|

**Brahms, Johannes (Cont.)**   Sonata No. 2 in A Major, Op. 100 (Cont.)   C 2   by outbreaks of intense passion. The first theme returns and is followed by lyric passages of great nobility. Throughout the movement there is a feeling of warmth and smoldering fire. A joyful coda brings the movement to an end.

Sonata No. 3 in D Minor, Op. 108   C 2   Allegro moderato ♩ = 74. The opening is introspect and dreamy, even hazy. A sudden forte introduces a section of great rhythmical virility and intense passion. It is followed by a theme of affectionate warmth. A playful dialogue leads to a mysterious and poetic development, and from there back to the first theme. The movement ends on a note of warmth and affection.

Adagio ♪=56. The opening is warm and full. A rubato upsweep leads into an enthusiastic forte, which gives way to an idea of tender affection. Now the piano joins the violin in singing the first theme. The character of the second half of the movement is like that of the first, only more intensely so. A dreamy coda ends the piece in a mood of contentment.

Un poco presto e con sentimento ♩ = 126. The opening is imploring and affectionate, suggesting tender sighs. The forte passages in the middle section are rhythmical and virile. A coda of elusive wistfulness ends this unique and imaginative movement.

Presto agitato ♪= 128. The opening is stormy and passionate, changing soon to
(Cont.)

Brahms, Johannes
(Cont.)

Sonata No. 3 in D
Minor, Op. 108 (Cont.)

C 2

playfulness. A broad song
of praise sets in and leads
through a pp. passage
(mysterioso) to a lyric and
affectionate theme. Syn-
copations bring back the
first theme by way of dashing and virile forte passages.
The development calls for
forceful rhythm. The agitato
requires all-consuming
fire and sweep.

Concerto in D Major,
Op. 77
(cadenzas by Joachim
and Kreisler)

C 3

Allegro non troppo ♩ = 108.
Themes of loftiness and
loveliness contrasted by
themes and passages of
great rhythmical strength
characterize this movement.
Of the numerous high points,
a few might be mentioned,
such as the subtle episode
after the warm C minor
theme in the middle of the
movement and the reappear-
ance of the D major theme
after the cadenza, in its
sublime, almost transfigured
character. A joyful coda
brings the movement to a
glorious end.

Adagio ♪ = 63. This move-
ment has an outspoken
pastoral character. The
middle part builds up to a
turbulent climax but returns
again to peace and contentment. As so often, Brahms
treats us to one of his in-
describable codas. Care
should be taken not to drag
this movement.

Allegro giocoso ma non
troppo vivace ♩ = 82. A
spirit of joy and virility
permeates this movement.
At times passages of playfulness and loveliness provide the necessary contrast.
After a short but brilliant
cadenza the poco più presto
in 6/8 rhythm brings this
great concerto to a trium-
phant close.

| COMPOSER | TITLE, KEY & OP. | GR. | REMARKS |
|---|---|---|---|
| Bruch, Max | Kol Nidre (Hebrew melody) Op. 47 | C 2 | Adagio ma non troppo, calls for eloquent singing, fervor and warmth. |
| | Scotch Fantasy, Op. 46 | C 3 | The themes are mostly Scottish folk songs. |
| | | | Grave ♩= 54, somber, like a funeral march. |
| | | | Adagio cantabile ♪= 88, full and rich. |
| | | | Allegro ♩ = 116, joyful and rhythmically alive. |
| | | | Andante sostenuto ♩ = 66, a folk song of great simplicity building up to great emotional warmth. |
| | | | Allegro guerriero ♩ = 100, warlike and brilliant. |
| | Concerto No. 1, in G Minor, Op. 26 | C 3 | Allegro moderato ♩= 94. After the two short cadenzas in the solo violin, the accompaniment introduces a most characteristic figure, which serves as a rhythmical background for this movement. The middle section introduces cantilenas of intense fervor. A general accelerando brings the movement to a brilliant climax. |
| | | | Adagio ♪= 59. A cantabile movement par excellence; also a movement of dramatic high lights and poetic moods. |
| | | | Allegro energico ♩= 88-92. Its main characteristic is flashy and decisive rhythm. There are also moments of affection and tenderness. |
| | Concerto No. 2 in D Minor, Op. 44 | C 3 | Adagio ma non troppo ♩= 58. The opening is intensely warm and expressive. The movement calls for imagination and rubato playing. (Cont.) |

| COMPOSER | TITLE, KEY & OP. | GR. | REMARKS |
|---|---|---|---|
| Bruch,Max (Cont.) | Concerto No. 2 in D Minor, Op. 44 (Cont.) | C 3 | The con passione section demands authority and dramatic fervor. The F major theme (tranquillo) and the following section call for a tone of pure gold, building up to great emotional intensity. The movement ends in a mood of religious exaltation. |
| | | | Allegro moderato (Recitativo) $\quad$ = 86. The solo opening suggests the call of a horn. A recitative of great imagination and bravura follows. The allegro = 90, calls for dramatic fire. |
| | | | Finale (Allegro molto). = 100-104. Verve and fire are its outstanding characteristics. The meno mossa = 84, demands passionate warmth. Gracefully flowing 16th passages and playful ideas follow. A brilliant and tumultuous ending brings the movement to a close. |
| Burleigh, Cecil | Moto Perpetuo, Op. 21, No. 4 | C 1 | For concert and studio. Featuring spiccato bowing. |
| | Wing Foo, Op. 1, No. 1 | A 3 | For pupils only. Featuring spiccato bowing. |
| | Fairy Sailing, Op. 31, No. 2 | C 1 | For concert and studio. Fast fleeting legato passages; also spiccato passages. |
| | Indian Dance, Op. 6, No. 4 | C 1 | For concert and studio. Sparkling and spirited; featuring spiccato bowing. |
| | Village Dance in G Major | C 1 | For concert and studio. Spirited and enthusiastic. |
| Burmester, Willy | A few of 30 pieces by old masters arranged by Willy Burmester. | | |
| | Rameau, Gavotte | B 2 | Gay and happy; the triplet section playful. |

| COMPOSER | TITLE, KEY & OP. | GR. | REMARKS |
|---|---|---|---|
| Burmester, Willy (Cont.) | Martini, Gavotte | B 2 | Graceful, featuring flying staccato. |
| | Beethoven, Menuett In E-flat No. 1 | C 1 | The moderato is singing. The trio features spiccato passages. |
| | Handel, Arioso | A 2 or C 1 | Sustained and legato. |
| | Bach, Air on the G String | C 2 | Sustained and singing |
| | Haydn,Menuett in F | C 1 | Sparkling and rhythmical; featuring spiccato bowing. |
| | Beethoven, Menuett in G No. 2 | B 3 or C 1 | The allegretto is graceful with rhythmical emphasis. The trio displays spiccato bowing. |
| | Mozart, Menuett in E flat No. 2 | B 2 | Quaint and graceful. |
| | Loeillet Menuett | B 2 | For students. In first, second and third positions. |
| | Dittersforf, German Dance | A 2 or B 1 | For students. Graceful and lively. |
| | Mattheson, Air on G String | C 1 | Expressive, broad and sustained. |
| | Karl, P. E. Bach, Menuett | B 2 or C 1 | Graceful and singing. |
| | Handel, Bourrée | A 2 | Allegretto, expressive but rhythmically alive. |
| | Rameau, Rigaudon | A 3 | Presto, featuring lively and detached 8th figurations. |
| | Kuhlau, Menuett | C 1 | Allegretto, graceful. |
| | Lully, Gavotte | C 1 | Graceful and rhythmical'y alive. Some spiccato bowing. |
| | Gluck, Menuett in F | A 2 or B 1 | Singing and expressive. |

| COMPOSER | TITLE, KEY & OP. | GR. | REMARKS |
|---|---|---|---|
| Burmester, Willy (Cont.) | Gossec, Gavotte | B 2 | Featuring sparkling spiccato bowings. |
| | Gossec, Tambourin | B 3 or C 1 | Featuring spiccato, martellé and spiccato bowing. |
| | Handel, Menuett in 3rds | C 2 | Featuring 3rds and other double stops. |
| Castelnuovo-Tedesco | Sea Murmurs (Heifetz) | C 1 | Sustained and with floating tone (sordino). |
| | Lark, Poem in Form of a rondo (Heifetz) | C 3 | A colorful piece; featuring trills, florid legato passages, sparkling ricochet bowing, harmonics, etc. |
| | Tango (Heifetz) | C 2 | Graceful with pointed rhythm; some double-stops and pizzicati. |
| Chaminade, Cécile | Serenade Española (Kreisler) | C 2 | Suave and charming, makes an excellent encore. |
| Chausson, Ernest | Poème, Op. 25 | C 3 | A most colorful and imaginative composition. Passages of dramatic intensity are contrasted with ideas of mystery and poetry. Its exotic harmonies are aglow with warmth and color. To do justice to this fascinating composition, the performer must have great imagination and sensitivity. |
| Chopin, Frédéric | Mazurka in A Minor (posthumous) (Kreisler) | C 2 | Charming and rhythmically flexible. |
| | Nocturne in E-flat Major transcribed from Op. 9, No. 2 by Sarasate (The same simplified by Ambrosio) | C 2 / A 2 | Suave and dreamy; also florid cadenzas. |
| | Nocturne, Op. 62, No. 1 (Kochanski) | C 2 | Singing and affectionate. Some florid passages. |
| | Nocturne No. 12 in C Major, Op. 37, No. 2 (Spalding) | C 3 | Featuring spiccato, ricochet, harmonics and double-stops. |

| COMPOSER | TITLE, KEY & OP. | GR. | REMARKS |
|---|---|---|---|
| Chopin, Frédéric (Cont.) | Waltz in B Minor, Op. 69, No. 2 (Spalding) | C 3 | Easy flowing, some double stops. |
| | Nocturne in E-flat, Op. 55, No. 2 (Heifetz) | C 2 | Sustained and singing. |
| | Nocturne in C-sharp Minor (posthumous) (Milstein) | C 2 | Poetic and dreamy; also long and graceful scale passages. |
| | Mazurka in A Major, Op. 33, No. 2 (Kreisler) | C 2 | Featuring flying staccato. |
| Cole, Ulric | Sonata for violin and piano | C 2 | Moderato. Although the opening theme in the violin is nostalgic in character, it must move at about the rate of a slow walk. There is no change in tempo in the second theme until one reaches a middle section marked animato, which calls for a slight increase in speed and continues up to a ritardando in the fourth bar, after letter E which reestablishes the original tempo. The piu mosso at letter G should be regarded conservatively since the piano figure in this section loses effectiveness and clarity if played too fast. At letter H, a slight ritardando (not indicated) helps to bring back the original tempo, in which the movement closes. |

Allegro molto. The sly, teasing character of the opening section of this scherzo should be played in a precise, even beat at a speed to allow accurate teamwork between the two instruments. The middle section, from letter B to letter D, changes in mood but not in tempo and should be played legato in both

(Cont.)

**Cole, Ulric (Cont.)** — Sonata for violin and piano (Cont.) — C 2 — instruments to form a contrast to the recapitulation which is again brisk and precise.

Andante <u>languido</u>. This movement, though slow, must not be allowed to drag. It should be played legato throughout with the exception of the two climactic spots, which require additional accentuation.

<u>Moderato</u>. This four-measure introduction is taken at about the same speed as the first movement. The principal theme (<u>allegro con brio</u>) must sound deliberate and controlled. At the sixteenth bar after letter C, a very slight ritard is helpful to lend emphasis to the climax in the following measure. At letter L, the <u>accelerando</u> should be achieved little by little in the following eight measures so as to arrive at the final <u>agitato</u> section at a speed which can still permit of further extension at the last three bars.

**Conus, Jules** — Concerto in E Minor — C 3 — <u>Allegro molto</u>♩ = 100-104. The solo violin starts with a tender and appealing <u>recitativo</u>. The following <u>andante</u> lends itself well to free declamation and builds up to the dramatic climax of the <u>poco più moderato</u> quasi tempo I. An intensely warm and melodic section follows. The <u>meno mosso</u> is fiery and intensly rhythmical. A brief cadenza leads to a lyric section of graceful, swaying character and builds up to great fervor. In the <u>andante</u> some of the opening ideas are recalled but in an intensified character. The <u>allegro tempo I</u> is very rhythmical and brilliant.

| COMPOSER | TITLE, KEY & OP. | GR. | REMARKS |
|---|---|---|---|
| Conus, Jules (Cont.) | Concerto in E Minor (Cont.) | C 3 | Adagio ♩= 65. The opening is singing and invites to free molding of the melodic line. The poco più mosso builds up in ever-growing intensity but gradually relaxes and ends on a dreamy note. What follows now is largely a repetition of the first solo section of the concerto. After the cadenza a few bars of andante lead to the brilliant and dashing end of this very "violinistic" concerto. |
| Corelli, Arcangelo | La Folia (Kreisler) | C 2 | Manifold variations of contrasting character on the broad and sustained theme. |
| | Variations on a theme by Corelli (Tartini-Kreisler) | C 1 | The theme is dignified and proud. Var. 1, light and florid. Var. 2, sparkling, featuring trills. Var. 3, featuring heavy chords. |
| Dancla, Jean Charles | Air with Variations, Op. 123, No. 7 | A 1 | For beginners. Very easy. |
| | Waltz, Op. 123, No. 2 | A 1 | For students only. Legato and singing. |
| | Petite Valse, Op. 48, No. 4 | A 2 | For students only. |
| | Six airs variés, Op. 89: | B 3 | All six airs represent fine teaching material for singing tone, double-stops, spiccato, staccato, ricochet, etc. |

1-Air varié on a theme by Pacini
2-Air    ”    ” ”    ”    ” Rossini
3-Air    ”    ” ”    ”    ˙ ” Bellini
4-Air    ”    ” ”    ”    ” Donizetti
5-Air    ”    ” ”    ”    ” Weigl
6-Air    ”    ” ”    ”    ” Mercadante

| COMPOSER | TITLE, KEY & OP. | GR. | REMARKS |
|---|---|---|---|
| | Résignation, morceau de Salon. Op. 59 | C 1 | A charming piece in the higher positions for more advanced students. Develops singing tone, has also florid cadenzas. |
| | Concert solo in B Minor, Op. 77, Nos. 1 and 3 | C 2 | Featuring singing tone, flowing passages, staccato runs, broad and vigorous (Cont.) |

| COMPOSER | TITLE, KEY & OP. | GR. | REMARKS |
| --- | --- | --- | --- |
| Dancla, Jean Charles (Cont.) | Concert Solo in B Minor, Op. 77, Nos.1 and 3 (Cont.) | C 2 | passages. Good teaching material. |
| Debussy, Claude | La Fille aux cheveux de lin (Hartmann) | C 1 | Imaginative and poetic. |
| | Clair de lune | C 1 | Sensitive and sustained (with sordino). |
| | Golliwogg s Cakewalk (Heifetz) | C 1 | Spirited and joyful; also decisive rhythm. |
| | Minstrels | C 2 | Featuring guitar effects. |
| | "La plus que lente" | C 1 | An imaginative rubato piece. |
| | Beau Soir (Heifetz) | C 1 | A singing piece (with sordino). |
| | En bateau (Choisnel) | C 1 | Easy flowing and singing. |
| | Mandoline ( A. Bachmann) | B 2 | Light and lively. |
| | Sonata for piano and violin in G Minor | C 2 | Allegro vivo ♩ = 55, elusive, restless and agitated. Intermede ♩ = 75, humorous and witty. Finale (trés animé), joyful and exuberant. |
| Dohnányi, Erno von | Ruralia Hungaria, Op. 32 | C 2 | Presto, featuring decisive rhythm and spiccato bowing. Andante rubato, free like an improvisation. Vivace, a lively dance featuring spiccato bowing. |
| Drdla, Franz | Serenade No. 1 in A | C 2 | For pupils only. Graceful and light; also some double-stops. |
| | The same simplified by Ambrosio | A 2 | |
| | Souvenir in D | C 1 | A graceful and popular piece. |
| | The same simplified by Ambrosio | A 1 | |

| COMPOSER | TITLE, KEY & OP. | GR. | REMARKS |
| --- | --- | --- | --- |
| Drigo, Riccardo | Serenade, from ballet "Les millions d'Arlequin"(Auer) | C 2 | Expressive and singing. |
| | The same simplified by Ambrosio | A 2 | |
| | Valse Bluette (Auer) | C 2 | Featuring sustained tone, spiccato and harmonics. |
| | The same simplified by Ambrosio | A 2 | |
| Dvořák, Anton | "Songs my mother taught me," Op. 55, No. 4 (Persinger) | C 2 | Singing and expressive; some double-stops. |
| | The same simplifed by Ambrosio | A 1 | |
| | Humoresque in G flat (Heifetz) | C 2 | Subtle, sensitive and singing; also double-stops. |
| | The same simplified by Ambrosio | A 2 | |
| | Sonatina in G Major Op. 100 | B 3 | For studio use. Stimulating by its pleasing sound, its interesting rhythms, and its colorful harmonies. |
| | Free transcriptions by Fritz Kreisler: | | |
| | Indian Lament | C 2 | Based on the Larghetto of Op. 100. |
| | Negro Spiritual, melody from the Largo of the "New World Symphony" | C 2 | Sustained and expressive; also double-stops. |
| | Slavonic Dance in G Minor No. 1 | C 2 | These three charming concert pieces express the melancholy and warmth of the Slavonic folk soul. Featuring double-stops. |
| | Slavonic Dance in E Minor No. 2 | | |
| | Slavonic Dance in G Major No. 3 | | |
| | Concerto in A Minor, Op. 53 | C 3 | Allegro ma non troppo ♩ = 108, a movement of sharp contrasts. Sections of challenge and defiance, |

| COMPOSER | TITLE, KEY & OP. | GR. | REMARKS |
|---|---|---|---|
| Dvořák, Anton (Cont.) | Concerto in A Minor, Op. 53 (Cont.) | C 3 | of romantic tenderness, of brilliant cadenzalike passages; also themes of Slavic fervor and carefree happiness provide the highlights of this colorful moment.<br><br>Adagio ma non troppo ♪= 60, a romantic, affectionate, wistful and imaginative movement inviting to rubato playing. "Happiness through tears" may best describe its character. The poco più mosso is decisive and challenging.<br><br>Finale (Allegro giocoso ma non troppo) ♩. = 104. The decisive and sparkling opening theme suggests joy and happiness. Playful 16th passages and strongly accentuated syncopations follow. Soon a gently swaying lyric section is introduced and provides a welcome contrast. Decisive rhythm and flashing brilliance return. The listlesso tempo brings a Slavic theme of crisp, wistful tenderness. This idea is enlarged upon in the bold 16th figurations of the solo violin. The tempo I brings back the opening idea and repeats the original pattern. The end of the movement builds up to a brilliant climax. |
| Elgar, Edward | La Capricieuse (Heifetz) | C 2 | Charming and graceful; featuring flying staccato. |
| | Salut d'amour, Op. 12 | C 1 | Singing, with a graceful sway. |
| | The same simplified by Ambrosio | A 2 | |

| COMPOSER | TITLE, KEY & OP. | GR. | REMARKS |
|---|---|---|---|
| Elgar, Edward (Cont.) | Violin concerto in B Minor, Op. 61 | C 3 | Allegro ♩= 100, noble and distinguished. The many tempo changes call for great elasticity and imagination.<br><br>Andante ♩= 52. A hymn of unassuming simplicity opens the movement and is later used as a background for the solo part. Sections of great loftiness and eloquence follow.<br><br>Allegro molto ♩= 138, spirited and brilliant; also has sections of noble singing and affectionate tenderness. After the cadenza, which recalls themes of the first movement, the concerto builds up to a grandiose ending. |
| Elman, Mischa | Concert Transcriptions: | | |
| | Grandmother's Minuet (Grieg) | C 1 | Light and graceful; featuring spiccato bowing. |
| | Après un Reve (Fauré) | C 2 | Singing and expressive, all on the G string. |
| | Deep River (old Negro melody) | C 2 | Singing and sustained; also double-stops. |
| | Etude Caprice (Rode) | C 2 | Featuring spiccato and staccato bowing. |
| | Song without words | C 2 | Singing and expressive. |
| | Tango (Albéniz) | C 2 | Rhythmically charming; also double-stops. |
| | Cradle Song (Schubert) | C 2 | Singing. Featuring double-stops and harmonics. |
| | "None but the Lonely Heart" (Tchaikovsky) | C 1 | Sustained and expressive; some double-stops. |
| | Serenade (Schubert) | C 2 | Singing and expressive; some florid variations and double-stops. |

| COMPOSER | TITLE, KEY & OP. | GR. | REMARKS |
|---|---|---|---|
| Ernst, Heinrich | Hungarian Melodies, Op. 22 | C 3 | Three charming Hungarian themes with variations offer opportunity for technical display such as scales in thirds, octaves, and tenths, harmonics, arpeggios, long scales in ricochet bowing, spiccato, etc. Rubato playing and singing tone also are called for. |
| | Concerto in F-sharp Minor, Op. 23 (Auer) | C 3 | Allegro moderato ♩ = 104, pompous and strutting. Excellent for developing technique. Its musical value is debatable. A very difficult piece. |
| Fauré, Gabriel | Sonata in A Major, Op. 13 | C 2 | Allegro ♩ = 126, sunny, romantic, enthusiastic; sometimes passionate, aglow with the joy of living. There are also poetic moments and moments of mystery. |
| | | | Andante ♩ = 56. The opening suggests a transparent, fleeting but reflective mood. Beginning with the espressivo, the character changes to one of fervor and animation, even passion. These contrasting moods interchange, creating moments of serene spirituality and high points of dramatic fervor. |
| | | | Allegro vivo ♩ = 152. The character of the opening is sparkling, effervescent, and playful. The 3/4 section is singing and expressive. |
| | | | Allegro quasi presto ♩. = 176. Its graceful, melodic flow is contrasted by syncopated phrases of driving passion. The end is brilliant and dashing. |

Franck, César     Sonata in A Major     C 2   Allegretto ben moderato ♪. = about 60. The opening conveys a mood of mystery and loftiness. The molto crescendo leads to a section of great breadth and exaltation, but gives way to noble and affectionate singing in the piano part. The opening idea returns and the pattern is repeated in a more intensified character. It is a movement of miraculous color and spiritual exaltation.

Allegro ♩ = 132. The opening is turbulent and passionate. The meno F is wooing and affectionate but soon gives way again to the appassionata character. A section of noble singing and caressing tenderness, of dreamy poetry and fiery passion follows. The movement ends on a note of triumph.

Recitativo-Fantasia (ben moderato) ♩ = 48, a movement of great flexibility in the tempo. The opening in the piano part suggests heartbreaking poignancy. The short rubato violin cadenza calls for authority and imagination. A dreamy dialogue follows and the plaintive recitativo phrase in the violin leads back to the opening idea. The molto tranquillo, an imaginative and mysterious section, is contrasted by the poco animato, which suggests great strength and authority. The section after the double bar starts in a dreamy mood but builds up to great dramatic fervor. Then follow moments of sublime exaltation and more dramatic outcries. The movement ends in a serious, reflective mood.

| COMPOSER | TITLE, KEY & OP. | GR. | REMARKS |
|---|---|---|---|
| Franck, César (Cont.) | Sonata in A Major (Cont.) | C 2 | Allegretto poco mosso ♩ = 88. The opening is sunny and friendly, but builds up to sweep and enthusiasm. A theme of the previous movement appears, alternating with the opening idea of the movement. A playful and fleeting section opens with the p subito. The B-flat minor section suggests caressing tenderness. It is being followed by passages of great strength and rhythmical virility. Another theme of the preceding movement comes back (ff.) in its full glory and grandeur. Gradually a quieter mood returns and brings back the opening theme. The movement ends in a mood of triumph and exultation. |
| Franko, Sam | Arrangements: | | |
| | A selection from composers of the 17th and 18th centuries | -- | Mostly for studio use. |
| | André Grétry Danse légère | B 2 | Light and graceful. |
| | Danse de Colinette | B 2 | Gay and lively; featuring spiccato bowing. |
| | Wolfgang A. Mozart Gavotte, from "Les petits Riens" | B 2 | Easy flowing. |
| | Pantomime, from "Les petits Riens" | B 2 | Light and graceful. |
| | Johann S. Bach Badinerie | B 2 | Temporarily out of print. |
| | Pierre Monsigny Rigaudon | C 1 | Spirited and gay. |
| | Antonio Sacchini Air de Dardames | B 2 | Singing and graceful. |

| COMPOSER | TITLE, KEY & OP. | GR. | REMARKS |
|---|---|---|---|
| Friedberg, Carl | Arrangements: | | |
| | Menuet by Haydn (Kreisler) | B 2 | Light and graceful. |
| | Adagio by Mozart (Kreisler) | C 2 | Singing and very expressive. |
| | Rondo by Schubert (Kreisler) | C 2 | Gay and lively, featuring spiccato passages; has moments of expressive tenderness. A charming piece for concert use. Excellent teaching material. |
| Gardner, Samuel | Troubadour | C 1 | Featuring spiccato and ricochet bowing. |
| | Preludes, Op. 14 | | |
| | 1. Prelude in B | C 2 | Molto largamente e sostenuto. |
| | 2. Prelude quasi improvisata | C 2 | Molto moderato. |
| | 3. Prelude in B Minor | C 2 | Andante con moto. |
| | 5. Prelude in G Minor | C 2 | Lento e placido (with mute). |
| | Coquetterie, Op. 26 | C 2 | Graceful and expressive; some double-stops. |
| | "From the cane brake," Op. 5, No. 1 | C 2 | Featuring Negro swing; has double-stops. |
| Gershwin, George | Three preludes (Heifetz) | C 2 | Prelude I, very rhythmical and jazzy; featuring double stops and spiccato. |
| | | | Prelude II, quietly singing (blues). |
| | | | Prelude III, wild and jazzy (double-stops). |
| Glazunov, Alexander | Caprice Variant (Godron) | C 1 | Featuring light spiccato bowing. |
| | Meditation (Heifetz) Op. 32 | C 2 | Singing and expressive. |
| | Mélodie Arabe (Kochanski) | C 1 | Vigorous and lively; also sustained and rich. |

| COMPOSER | TITLE, KEY & OP. | GR. | REMARKS |
|---|---|---|---|
| Glazunov, Alexander (Cont.) | Serenade Espagnole (Kreisler) | C 1 | Easy flowing and graceful. |
| | Concerto in A Minor, Op. 82 (Auer) | C 3 | Moderato ♩ = 92, warm affectionate and imaginative; at times passionate and brilliant. |
| | | | Andante ♩ = 58, eloquent and intensely warm, building up to passionate fervor, but drifting back by way of an imaginative and poetic passage to tempo 1. After a brief orchestra tutti comes a brilliant display of the solo violin. The opening theme of the concerto returns in double-stops, embellished somewhat, and a brilliant cadenza leads to the |
| | | | Allegro ♩= 84-88. The opening theme is extremely rhythmical in character. The grazioso after the double bar is friendly, affectionate and graceful. With the animato it changes to a more dashing character. A short tutti leads to the extremely rhythmical "Cossack" theme in D major. Evermore intensifying, the movement builds up to a brilliant end. |
| Gluck, Christoph W. von | Dance of the Blessed Spirits, Minuet from Orpheus (Ambrosio) | A 1 | Serene and easy flowing. |
| | Musette from "Armide" | B 2 | For studio, light and graceful. |
| | Gavotte, from Iphigenia in Aulis (Hartmann) | B 2 | Graceful. |
| | Gavotte in A (Burmester) | C 1 | Easy flowing and graceful; spiccato bowing. |
| | Mélodie (Kreisler) | C 2 | Sustained and expressive. |

| COMPOSER | TITLE, KEY & OP. | GR. | REMARKS |
|---|---|---|---|
| Godard, Benjamin | Berceuse, from Jocelyn | C 1 | Sustained and singing. |
| | The same simplified | A 2 | |
| | Au Matin, Op. 83 | B 2 | Singing and easy flowing. |
| | Canzonetta, from "Concert Romantique," Op. 36 | B 2 | Featuring light bow and flying staccato. |
| | Adagio pathétique, Op. 128, No. 3 (in B-flat) | C 2 | Broad and singing. |
| Godowsky, Leopold | Transcriptions: | | |
| | Alt Wien (Heifetz) | C 2 | Singing, persuasive and caressing; some double-stops. |
| | Swan (Saint-Saëns) | C 2 | Serene and sustained. |
| | Waltz Poem No. 1 | C 2 | Suave and amiable. Some double-stops. |
| Goldmark, Carl | Concerto Op. 28 in A Minor | C 3 | Allegro moderato ♩ = 112, lyric and romantic; a singing piece, par excellence. Brilliant passages provide welcome contrast. |
| | | | Andante ♩ = 66, tenderly singing, the poco animato in G minor builds up to great dramatic fervor. An excellent piece for tone. |
| | | | Allegretto ♩ = 112, fiery rhythm, dashing passage-work, and melodies of great fervor are featured in this movement. |
| Goldmark, Rubin | The Call of the Plains | C 2 | Moderato, sustained and singing. |
| | Witches' Sabbath | C 2 | Featuring brilliant 16th figurations. |
| Gossec, F. J. | Gavotte (Burmester) | B 3 | Featuring spiccato and ricochet bowing. |
| Gounod, Charles | Ava Maria, meditation on the first prelude by Bach | B 3 | Featuring sustained tone. |

| COMPOSER | TITLE, KEY & OP. | GR. | REMARKS |
| --- | --- | --- | --- |
| Gounod, Charles (Cont.) | Ava Maria, meditation on the first prelude by Bach (Cont.) | | |
| | The same simplified by Ambrosio | A 1 | |
| | March in C, from Faust (Soldiers' Chorus) | A 2 | For studio. |
| | Flower Song, from Faust | B 1 | For studio. |
| Grainger, Percy | "Molly on the Shore" (Irish reel) (Kreisler) | C 2 | Featuring spiccato bowing. |
| Granados, Enrique | Spanish Dance (Kreisler) | C 2 | Featuring double-stops and interesting accompaniment rhythm. |
| | Intermezzo, from Goyescas (S. Jacobson) | C 2 | Broad and singing. Featuring also spiccato, harmonics, pizzicati, trills, etc. |
| Grasse, Edwin | Wellenspiel (Waves at Play) | C 3 | Fast legato passages, mostly scales. |
| Grieg, Edvard | Norwegian Dance, Op. 35, No. 2 | C 1 | For students only. Has a graceful sway. |
| | Last Spring (Saenger) | C 1 | For students only. Smooth and singing. |
| | Peer Gynt Suite No. 1, Op. 46 | | |
| | Death of Åse | C 1 | For pupils only. Slow, sad and sustained. |
| | Anitra's Dance | C 1 | For students only, light and graceful. |
| | Puck (Kobold) Op. 71, No. 3 (Achron) | C 1 | Featuring spiccato, double-stops, and harmonics. |
| | Solvejg's song (Brown and Hubay) | C 1 | For pupils only. Singing and graceful. |
| | Sonata No. 1 in F, Op. 8 | C 2 | Allegro con brio ♩ = 80-84, easy flowing, breathing joy of living. The andante suggests a touch of sadness. |

| COMPOSER | TITLE, KEY & OP. | GR. | REMARKS |
|---|---|---|---|
| Grieg, Edvard (Cont.) | Sonata No. 1 in F, Op. 8 (Cont.) | C 2 | Allegretto quasi andantino ♩ = 126-132, graceful and friendly; sometimes flirtatious, sometimes pompous. The più vivo suggests a joyful dance.<br><br>Allegro molto vivace ♩ = 132, brilliant and rhythmically crisp; also persuasive and graceful. |
| | Sonata No. 3 in C Minor, Op. 45 (Spiering) | C 2 | Allegro molto ed appassionato ♩. = 112-116, passionate and brilliant; also mysterious and singing. In short, very colorful.<br><br>Allegretto espressivo alla romanza ♩ = 88, a love song. Allegro molto ♩ = 144, pointed and sparkling.<br><br>Allegro animato ♩ = 112, suggests the dancing of a gnome. Cantabile ♩ = 95-100, broad, with great fervor. |
| Handel, George F. | Largo | C 1 | Featuring broad and sustained bowing. |
| | Simplified by Ambrosio | A 1 or A 2 | |
| | Larghetto (Willeke) | C 1 | Sustained and singing. |
| | Transcriptions by Carl Flesch: | | |
| | Aria ("He shall feed his flock") | C 1 | Temporarily out of print. |
| | Aria ("O had I Jubal's lyre"), from "Joshua" | C 1 | Jubilant and happy. |
| | Prayer ("Vouchsafe, O Lord"), from the "Te Deum" | C 1 | Broad and sustained. |
| | Lamento ("Who calls my parting soul"), from "Ester" | C 2 | Sustained and with fervor; some double-stops. |

| COMPOSER | TITLE, KEY & OP. | GR. | REMARKS |
|---|---|---|---|
| Handel, George F. (Cont). | Transcriptions by Carl Flesch: (Cont.) | | |
| | Pastorale ("Beneath the vine"), from "Solomon" | C 2 | Graceful and smooth. |
| | Arioso (Burmester) | A 2 or C 1 | For pupils only. Sustained bowings. |
| | Bourree (Burmester) | A 2 | For pupils only. Easy flowing but expressive. |
| | Menuet (Burmester) | B 2 | Proud and authoritative. |
| | Six Sonatas | | |
| | (Auer-Friedberg) Sonata No. 1, in A Major | C 1 | Andante ♪ = 70, singing and warmhearted. |
| | | | Allegro ♩ = 120, joyful and rhythmically decisive. |
| | | | Adagio ♪ = 52, eloquent. |
| | | | Allegro ♩. = 88, amiable and friendly. |
| | Sonata No. 2, in G Minor | C 1 | Andante ♪ = 68, eloquent and dignified. |
| | | | Allegro ♩ = 112, gay, at times playful . |
| | | | Adagio ♪ = 88, sustained; with intense warmth. |
| | | | Allegretto ♩. = 92, graceful and playful. |
| | Sonata No. 3, in F Major | C 1 | Adagio ♩ = 54, lofty and eloquent. |
| | | | Allegro ♩ = 115, wide awake and very alive. |
| | | | Largo ♩ = 48, sustained and singing. |
| | | | Allegro ♩. = 117, playful and alive. |

| COMPOSER | TITLE, KEY & OP. | GR. | REMARKS |
| --- | --- | --- | --- |
| Handel, George F. (Cont.) | Six Sonatas (Cont.) | | |
| | Sonata No. 4, in D Major | C 1 | Adagio ♪ = 66, eloquent, noble, and dignified. |
| | | | Allegro ♩ = 116, gay and rhythmically decisive. |
| | | | Larghetto ♪ = 70, sustained and with great fervor. |
| | | | Allegro ♩ = 110, jubilant and rhythmically alive. |
| | Sonata No. 5, in A Major | C 1 | Adagio ♪ = 70-72, lofty and noble. |
| | | | Allegro ♩ = 104, gay and festive. |
| | | | Largo ♩ = 48, noble and eloquent. |
| | | | Allegro ♩. = 60, brilliant and gay. |
| | Sonata No. 6, in E Major | C 1 | Adagio ♪ = 80-84, sustained and singing. |
| | | | Allegro ♩ = 102, suggesting a happy sway. |
| | | | Largo ♩ = 82, noble and broad. |
| | | | Allegro ♩. = 70, happy and playful. |
| Harris, Roy | Dance of Spring | C 1 | A medium short piece with a graceful swing. |
| | Fantansy | C 1 | A medium short piece of eloquent and powerful character. |
| | Melody | C 1 | A slow, sustained piece; building up to an intense climax in the middle section. |

| COMPOSER | TITLE, KEY & OP. | GR. | REMARKS |
|---|---|---|---|
| Hartmann, Arthur | Tiny Suite for Tiny Fiddlers; | | |
| | March of the A-B-C-'s | A 1 | This suite features all kinds of violinistic problems for the beginner. |
| | One-Finger Waltz | A 1 | |
| | See-Saw | A 1 | |
| | Transcriptions: | | |
| | A la Viennoise (J. Brandl) | C 1 | Double-stops and spiccato; also lyric sections. |
| | Albumleaf (Grieg) | C 1 | Featuring crisp rhythm. |
| | Autumn Song (Tchaikovsky) | C 1 | Singing, in a doleful mood. |
| | Chanson Triste (Tchaikovsky) | A 1 or B 3 | For pupils only. A simple melody. |
| | Mazurka (Chopin) | B 2 | Featuring flying staccato. |
| | Nocturne (Fauré) | C 1 | Singing (use of mute). |
| Hauser, Miska | Cradle-song in A Major, Op. 11 No. 2 | B 2 | For pupils only. Simple and singing. |
| Haydn, Joseph | Menuetto in F | B 2 | Light and graceful bowing. |
| | Andantino Grazioso, from String Quartet Op. 3, No. 1 (Pochon) | B 2 | For pupils. Graceful and friendly. |
| | Serenade (Auer) | B 3 | For pupils. Singing and friendly. |
| | Menuet in C Major (Hartmann) | B 2 | Graceful and dignified; trio smooth. |
| | Vivace (Auer) | C 2 | Featuring fast spiccato bowing. |
| | Adagio and Presto (Heifetz) | C 2 | Adagio, broad and dignified. Presto, light; featuring spiccato bowing. |
| | Hungarian Rondo (Kreisler) | C 2 | Featuring fast spiccato bowing and decisive rhythm. |

| COMPOSER | TITLE, KEY & OP. | GR. | REMARKS |
|----------|-----------------|-----|---------|
| Haydn, Joseph (Cont.) | Divertimento (transcribed by Piatigorsky and Elkan) | B 3 | Adagio ♪ = 92, singing and affectionate. |
| | | | Menuet ♩ = 165, graceful and light. |
| | | | Allegro di molto ♩ = 138, gay and lively. |
| Heifetz, Jascha | Ao pé da fogueria (Valle) | C 1 | South American character piece in double-stops. |
| | Ave Maria (Schubert) | C 1 | Sustained and singing; also octaves and other double-stops. |
| | Estralita (My Little Star) (Ponce) | C 1 | Sweet and singing. |
| | Hebrew Lullaby (Achron) | C 1 | A tender and dreamy melody (use of mute). |
| | Hebrew Dance (Achron) | C 2 | Featuring cadenzas, spiccato, trills, florid legato passages, and double-stops. |
| | Huella (Aguirre) | C 1 | South American piece, has octaves and other double-stops. |
| | Larghetto, from the Concerto for String Orchestra (Vivaldi) | C 1 | Singing and expressive. |
| | Rigaudon (Rameau) | C 1 | Featuring graceful and light bowing. |
| | Transcriptions: | | |
| | Alt Wien (Godowsky) | C 2 | Tender and caressing; inviting to rubato playing. |
| | Beau Soir (Debussy) | C 2 | Sustained and singing. |
| | Bumble Bee (Rimsky-Korsakov) | C 2 | Featuring fast spiccato bowing, mostly in chromatics. |
| | Deep River (Negro Spiritual) | C 2 | Slow, broad and singing, also double-stops. |
| | Fileuse (Spinning Song) (Popper) | C 2 | Fast flowing triplet figuration (legato). |

| COMPOSER | TITLE, KEY & OP. | GR. | REMARKS |
|---|---|---|---|
| Heifetz, Jascha (Cont.) | Transcriptions, (Cont.) | | |
| | Gavotte (Prokofieff), Op. 32 | C 2 | Graceful but rhythmical precision; also double-stops. |
| | Gavotte and Musette (Bach) | C 2 | Graceful and smooth. |
| | Guitarre, Op. 45, No. 2 (Moszkowski-Sarasate) | C 2 | Featuring double-stops, harmonics, spiccato, pizzicato and florid passages. |
| | Hora Staccato (Dinicu) | C 2 | A fast piece, featuring long and brilliant staccato runs. |
| | Hungarian Dance No. 7 (Brahms-Joachim) | C 2 | See under Brahms. |
| | Larghetto and Gavotte from Classical Symphony (Prokofieff) | C 2 | Larghetto, sustained and singing. Gavotte, humorous but somewhat heavy. |
| | Lark (Poem in form of a rondo) (Castelnuovo-Tedesco) | C 2 | See under Castelnuovo-Tedesco. |
| | Malagueña (Sarasate) | C 2 | See under Sarasate. |
| | March, from The Love for Three Oranges (Prokofieff) | C 2 | See under Prokofieff. |
| | On Wings of Song, Op. 34, No. 2 (Mendelssohn-Achron) | C 2 | Singing and expressive; also double-stops. |
| | Bird as Prophet, Op. 82 (Schumann) | C 2 | Lento, whimsical and fantastic. Meno mosso, expressive (double-stops). |
| | Rondo in E-flat (Hummel) | C 2 | Light and graceful; some double-stops. |
| | Rondo (Weber) | C 2 | Featuring fast and fleeting 16th passages; also spiccato bowing. |
| | Scherzo, from Midsummer Night's Dream (Mendelssohn) | C 2 | Featuring fast and light spiccato bowing. |

| COMPOSER | TITLE, KEY & OP. | GR. | REMARKS |
|---|---|---|---|
| Heifetz, Jascha (Cont.) | Transcriptions, (Cont.) | | |
| | Toccata (Paradise) | C 2 | Featuring fast 16th passages. A brilliant piece. |
| | Zapateado (Sarasate) | C 2 | A fast piece in 6/8 rhythm, featuring spiccato bowing. |
| | Presto in B-flat (Poulenc) | C 2 | Presto possibile, featuring spiccato bowing. |
| | Menuet in D (Mozart) | C 1 | Graceful; middle section featuring flying staccato. |
| | La Capricieuse (Elgar) | C 2 | Featuring flying staccato and double-stops. |
| Herbert, Victor | Serenade, from Suite, Op. 3 | C 2 | Graceful and charming; some double-stops. |
| | The same simplified by Ambrosio | A 2 | |
| | A la valse | C 2 | Featuring flying staccato and spiccato. |
| | Canzonetta in B-flat, Op. 12, No. 4 | C 1 | Graceful, featuring light spiccato bowing. |
| | Mirage | C 2 | Singing and expressive. |
| Hindemith, Paul | Concerto (1939) | C 3 | In moderately fast half-notes, $\d$=92-100, strong, virile and restless. |
| | | | Slow, quarters not faster than 40, serious and dignified; figuration passages very imaginative. |
| | | | Lively ♩ = 152, witty and gay. |
| Hochstein, David | Minuet in Olden Style | C 1 | Featuring spiccato and flying staccato. |
| | Waltz in A Major (original in A-flat Major) (Brahms) | C 2 | Tender and affectionate, featuring double-stops. |
| Hubay, Jenö | Hejre Kati (Czardas Scenes), Op. 32, No.4 | C 2 | A piece in Hungarian character, featuring spiccato bowing, trills, double-stops etc.; also sections of imaginative rubato playing. |

| --- | --- | --- | --- |
| Hubay, Jenö (Cont.) | Zephyr, Op. 30, No. 5 | C 2 | Featuring flying staccato, ricochet bowing and harmonics. |
| Huber, A. | Pupils' Concertino Op. 8, No. 4 | A 2 | Allegro moderato, featuring singing tone and fast passages. The middle section in 6/8 rhythm is graceful. |
| | Student Concerto No. 2, in G, Op. 6 | B 2 | Allegro moderato, featuring decisive rhythm and detached bowing; also singing sections.<br><br>Andante, graceful and expressive.<br><br>Allegro, featuring decisive rhythm and staccato runs; also spiccato passages. |
| Hubermann, Bronislaw | Transcriptions; | | |
| | Valse No. 2 of Op. 64 (Chopin) | C 2 | Featuring smooth legato passages and spiccato figurations. |
| | Valse, Op. 70, No. 1 (Chopin) | C 2 | Featuring big position shifts, also double-stops. |
| Jacobson, S. | Transcription: | | |
| | Cradle-Song (Tchaikovsky) | C 2 | Featuring florid cadenzas, and double-stops. |
| Jacobi, Frederick | Three Preludes | C 1 | 1. Lento non troppo.<br>2. Furioso.<br>3. Con movimento dolce.<br>Very short pieces, strongly contrasted in mood. |
| | Ballad for Violin and piano | C 3 | A virtuoso piece for both the violin and the piano, whose moods range from the tender to the dramatic. |
| | Violin Concerto (1937) (cadenza by Albert Spalding) | C 3 | A romantic work, well written for the violin. |
| Joachim, Joseph | Variations in E Minor for orchestra and violin | C 3 | Violinistically very interesting. Fine music, undeservedly neglected. |

| COMPOSER | TITLE, KEY & OP. | GR. | REMARKS |
|---|---|---|---|
| Joachim, Joseph (Cont.) | Hungarian Concerto in D Minor | C 3 | One of the most difficult concertos. Its length (over an hour) makes a performance in its entirety impracticable. The slow movement (Romanza) can be played separately. It is imaginative and tender, at times dramatic. A very effective piece. A la zingara describes the character of the last movement. |
| Kochanski, Paul | Mélodie Arabe (Glazunov) | C 1 | Featuring double-stops. |
| | Danse Sauvage | C 2 | Featuring fingered octaves and other double-stops. |
| | Flight (Caprice) | C 2 | Imaginative and colorful. |
| | Impromptu, Op. 90, No. 4 (Schubert) | C 2 | Light legato 16th passages. |
| | L'Aube (Dawn) | C 2 | Sustained, use of sordino, also double-stops. |
| | Jota, from Suite Populaire Espagnole (De Falla) | C 2 | Lively and rhythmically crisp; featuring pizzicato and ponticello; has also melodic sections. |
| Kramer, A. Walter | In Elizabethian Days (old English dance), Op. 32, No. 2 | B 2 | A quaint and graceful piece. Featuring pointed rhythm. |
| | Chant Nègre, Op. 32 No. 1 | C 1 | Slow and singing; a few double-stops. |
| | Gavotte, Op. 8, No. 1 | B 3 | Featuring light spiccato bowing. |
| | Transcriptions: | | |
| | "Like melodies arising" (Brahms) | C 1 | Singing and tender; has moments of great fervor. |
| | "Deep River" | C 1 | Singing and expressive; has double-stops. |
| Kreisler, Fritz | Original Compositions: | | |
| | Caprice Viennois | C 2 | The allegro moderato ♩ = 74 and the andante con moto ♩ = 56 are imaginative and (Cont.) |

| COMPOSER | TITLE, KEY & OP. | GR. | REMARKS |
|---|---|---|---|
| Kreisler, Fritz (Cont.) | Caprice Viennois (Cont.) | C 2 | free; the piu lento ♩ = 108 in the andante con moto (3/4 time) is wistful and tender. The Presto ♩,= 104 is capricious, brilliant and witty. |
| | Sicilienne and Rigaudon | C 2 | Tempo di allegretto, graceful with an easy sway. Rigaudon, featuring lively 16th passages in legato, and spiccato bowing. |
| | Tambourin Chinois | C 3 | Spirited and sparkling. |
| | Liebesfreud (Love's joy) | C 3 | Featuring virile rhythm and graceful charm. |
| | The same simplified | A 2 | |
| | Allegretto in G Minor | B 3 | Featuring flying staccato. |
| | La Précieuse | B 3 | Graceful and light; some flying staccato and brilliant trills. |
| | Menuet (in the style of Porpora) | B 3 | Allegro, stately and proud. The trio is graceful and easy flowing. |
| | Andantino | C 1 | Friendly and singing. |
| | Liebesleid | C 1 | Love's sorrow. |
| | Preghiera | C 1 | Singing and expressive. |
| | Scherzo | C 1 | Graceful, featuring flying staccato and trills. |
| | Recitativo and Scherzo for violin alone | C 2 | Recitativo (Lento con espressione), featuring rubato playing, double-stops, tremolo accompaniments, etc. Scherzo (Presto e brilliante), featuring spiccato bowing and double-stops. |
| | Allegretto in G Minor | C 2 | Requires decisive rhythm, featuring trills and spiccato. |
| | Aubade Provençale | C 2 | Andante, easy flowing. Allegro ma non troppo, rhythmically decisive. |

| Composer | Title, Key & Op. | Gr. | Remarks |
|---|---|---|---|
| Kreisler, Fritz (Cont.) | La Gitana (Arab-Spanish gypsy song of the 18th century) | C 2 | Proud;  also persuasive and graceful. |
| | Frascita (Lehar) | C 2 | Featuring flying staccato. |
| | La Chasse (caprice) (Cartier) | C 2 | Featuring spiccato and double-stops in a spirited 6/8 rhythm. |
| | Preludium and Allegro (in the style of Pugnani) | C 2 | Excellent for developing breadth of style and bow dexterity. |
| | Schoen Rosmarin | C 2 | Featuring flying staccato and spiccato;  a most graceful piece. |

Transcriptions and editions by Fritz Kreisler:

| | | | |
|---|---|---|---|
| | Ballet music from Rosamunde (Schubert) | C 2 | Calls for crisp rhythm and caressing persuasiveness. Also featuring double-stops. |
| | The Bell (La Campanella), from Concerto No. 2, Op. 7 (Paganini) | C 3 | Featuring spiccato, ricochet, trills, double stops and generally brilliant passage-work. |
| | Caprice No. 13 (Paganini) | C 3 | See under Paganini |
| | Caprice No. 20 (Paganini) | C 3 | ,, ,, ,, |
| | Caprice No. 24 (Paganini) | C 3 | ,, ,, ,, |
| | Caprice in A Minor (Wieniawski) | C 3 | Featuring spiccato bowing in 6/8 rhythm. |
| | Fantasie in C Major, Op. 131 (Schumann) | C 3 | See under Schumann. |
| | Fugue in A (Tartini) | C 1 | Dignified and severe;  many double-stops. |
| | Hymn to the Sun, from Le Coq d' Or (Rimsky-Korsakov) | C 2 | Oriental in flavor, a charming concert piece. |
| | Midnight bells, from The Opera Ball | C 1 | Tenderly singing;  some double-stops. |

| COMPOSER | TITLE, KEY & OP. | GR. | REMARKS |
|---|---|---|---|
| Kreisler, Fritz (Cont.) | Moment Musical Op. 94, No. 3 (Schubert) | C 2 | Charming, witty and rhythmically crisp; some double-stops. |
| | Chanson Louis 13th and Pavane | B 2 | Andante, in the character of a simple folk song. Allegretto, suggests crisp rhythm and a graceful sway. |
| | Rondino (Beethoven) | B 3 | Easy flowing and graceful. |
| | Mélodie (Gluck) | C 1 | Expressive and singing. |
| | Dance Espagnole, from La Vida Breve (De Falla) | C 1 | Rhythmically decisive, at times even pompous; has also moments of persuasiveness. |
| | Airs Russe, Souvenir de Moscou (Wieniawski) | C 3 | After a brilliant cadenza follows a simple Russian folk song with variations. Var. 1. Florid 16th passages Var. 2. (Lento) featuring harmonics. The allegro energico follows with another Russian theme of a decisive, at times exuberant character. A meno mosso in harmonics provides for contrast. |
| | Scherzo (Tchaikovsky) | C 1 | Presto giocoso, sparkling spiccato passages in 6/8 time. The middle section is legato and very expressive. |
| Kroll, W. | Three pieces in the first position with piano accompaniment or optional second violin accompaniment: | | |
| | Donkey Doodle | A 3 | Allegretto ♩ = 108, gay and lively. |
| | Contra Dance | A 3 | Poco allegro ♩ = 152-160, graceful and light. |
| | Peter Rabbit | A 3 | Molto vivace ♩ = 168, Excellent for left hand. |
| | | | All three pieces offer stimulating teaching material. |

**Kroll, W. (Cont.)** — Recital pieces:

Arabesque — C 2 — Andantino ♩ = 50, wistful and easy flowing.

Banjo and Fiddle — C 2 — Vivace ♩ = 144, gay and spirited, featuring banjo effects by pizzicati.

Juanita — C 1 — Vivace ♪ = 112, suave and and easy flowing.

Prayer — C 1 — Adagio ♩ = 40, fervently expressive and sustained.

**Lalo, Edouard** — Symphony Espagnole, Op. 21 — C 3 — Allegro non troppo ♩ = 82-84. Decisive rhythm, broad melodies of dramatic fervor, and moments of dreamy poetry lend the background to this colorful movement.

Scherzando ♪ = 200. Melodic charm, playfulness, brilliant and sparkling passages, a touch of sadness in the poco più lento are the characteristics of this movement, which has a distinctly Spanish flavor.

Intermezzo ♪ = 76, pompous, at times persuasive. The middle section is florid and brilliant.

Andante ♩ = 63. The opening solo is warm and intense. The second solo entrance builds up to dramatic fervor and passion, but gives way to poetic thoughtfulness. A movement of great emotional contrasts.

Rondo (Allegro ♩ = 108-112). Rhythmical decisiveness, brilliant passages, scintillating spiccato figurations lend the background to this movement. The rich and full cantilena of the first poco più lento ♩ = 84 and (Cont.)

| COMPOSER | TITLE, KEY & OP. | GR. | REMARKS |
|---|---|---|---|
| Lalo Edouard (Cont.) | Symphony Espagnole, Op. 21 (Cont.) | C 3 | the second poco più lento ♩ = 80 being passionate and ardent, caressing and per-suasive, provide a welcome contrast. The movement ends in a blaze of fireworks and dashing brilliancy. |
| Leclair, Jean Marie | Sonata "Le Tombeau" (F. David) | C 2 | Grave ♪ = 58, serious and eloquent.<br><br>Allegro ma non troppo ♩ = 69, playful and easy flow-ing.<br><br>Gavotte (Allegretto grazioso) ♩ = 54-58, light and graceful.<br><br>Allegro ♪· = 76, gay and and spirited. |
| Locatelli Pietro | Sonata in G Minor (Sauret) | C 1 | Largo ♩ = 56, serious, dig-nified and warm.<br><br>Allemanda ♩ = 100, stately but flowing.<br><br>Andante ♪ = 92, affectionate, warm and singing.<br><br>Allegretto ♩· = 92, spirited and easy flowing. |
| Loeffler, Charles M. | Adieu pour jamais (J. Gordon) | C 1 | Singing and expressive, building up to great fervor and warmth. |
|  | Les Paons (J. Gordon) | C 2 | Descriptive and imagina-tive, picturing the shim-mering and exotic colors of the peacock. |
| Martini, Giovanni B. | Sonata No. 1, in D (Endicott-Spalding) | B 3 | Allegro ♩ = 112, gay, play-ful and sunny.<br><br>Andante ♪ = 84, friendly and graceful.<br><br>Giocoso ♩ = 110, proud and joyful.<br><br>Presto ♩· = 72, spirited and gay.<br><br>(Mostly for students.) |

| COMPOSER | TITLE, KEY & OP. | GR. | REMARKS |
|---|---|---|---|
| Mascagni, Pietro | Intermezzo, from Cavalleria Rusticana | C 1 | For pupils only, featuring singing tone. |
| | The same simplified by Ambrosio | A 1 | |
| Mason, Daniel G. | Sonata in G Minor, Op. 5 | C 2 | Allegro moderato ♩ = 126, Romantic and singing. |
| | | | Andante traquillo, non troppo lento ♩ = 72. Warm-hearted and eloquent. |
| | | | Allegro vivace ♩.= 84, spir-ited and with great sweep. |
| Massenet, Jules | Elegy (Melody), Op. 10 | C 1 | Mostly for pupils. Featur-ing legato and singing tone. |
| | The same simplified by Ambrosio | A 1 | |
| | Last Dream of the Virgin, from "La Vierge" | C 1 | For pupils only; featuring sustained and singing tone. |
| Mendelssohn, Felix | Spring Song | B 2 | Mostly for pupils. Grace-ful and easy flowing. |
| | The same simplified by Ambrosio | A 1 | |
| | Wedding March, from Midsummer Night's Dream | B 3 | For pupils only. |
| | Capricietto (Canzonetta) | C 1 | Featuring light bowing and spiccato bowing. |
| | Song without Words (Kreisler) | C 2 | Sustained and affectionate, all on the G string. |
| | Concerto in E Minor, Op. 64 | C 3 | Allegro molto appassionato ♩ = 96. Emotional fervor, brilliant passages, poetic moments provide the back-ground for this warm and colorful movement. |
| | | | Andante ♪ =98. The open-ing cantilena is of serene beauty. The middle section develops great dramatic fervor. The first theme re-(Cont.) |

| COMPOSER | TITLE, KEY & OP. | GR. | REMARKS |
| --- | --- | --- | --- |
| Mendelssohn, Felix (Cont.) | Concerto in E Minor, Op. 64 (Cont.) | C 3 | turns but in a more spiritual character than at the beginning of the movement. The movement ends in a mood of peace and contentment. |
| | | | Allegretto non troppo $\quad$ =96-76, a section of great emotional fervor; hope alternating with despair. |
| | | | Allegro molto vivace $\quad$ = 186, sparkling, humorous and playful; ending in a triumphant climax. |
| Milhaud, Darius | Saudades do Brazil (Cl. Levy) | | |
| | 1.  Leine | C 1 | Six charming character |
| | 2.  Copacabana | C 1 | pieces. |
| | 3.  Ipanema | C 1 | |
| | 4.  Carcovado | C 1 | |
| | 5.  Tijiuca | C 1 | |
| | 6.  Sumare | C 1 | |
| Mozart, Wolfgang A. | Two easy minuets from the Viennese Sonatinas; arranged by G. Ross | B 1 | For pupils only. |
| | Gavotte, from "Les petits Riens" | B 2 | See under Franko. |
| | Gavotte in G (Auer) | B 2 | Suggests a graceful sway. |
| | Ländler (F. Ries) | A 2 | For pupils only.  Graceful and easy flowing. |
| | Minuet in D Major (Heifetz) | C 2 | Featuring spiccato, flying staccato, and trills. |
| | Adagio in E Major (F. Herman) (Köchel No. 261) | C 1 | Adagio $\quad$= 69, singing, serene, and affectionate. |
| | Eighteen sonatas for piano and violin | | |
| | Sonata No. 1, in A Major (Köchel No. 305) | B 2 | Allegro di molto $\quad$= 116, joyful and happy, calling for crisp rhythm. |

| COMPOSER | TITLE, KEY & OP. | GR. | REMARKS |
|---|---|---|---|
| Mozart, Wolfgang A. (Cont.) | Sonata No. 1, in A Major (Köchel No. 305) (Cont.) | B 2 | Andante grazioso ♪ = 100 (Tema con variazioni) The theme is friendly and graceful. |
| | | | Var. 1, fluid. Var. 2, sunny, friendly and content. Var. 3, easy flowing. Var. 4, exuberant and happy. Var. 5, stern and serious. Var. 6, (Allegro ♪ = 184), joyful and happy. |
| | Sonata No. 2 in C Major (Köchel No. 303) | B 2 | Adagio ♩ = 76-80, sunny, graceful and singing. |
| | | | Allegro molto ♩ = 94, light-footed and nimble. |
| | | | Tempo di menuetto ♩ = 100-108, graceful, polite and easy flowing. |
| | Sonata No. 3 in D Major (Köchel, No. 306) | B 2 | Allegro con spirito ♩ = 138, festive and joyful. |
| | | | Andante cantabile ♩ = 56-60. The first section is mild and singing. In the second section after the double bar, stateliness is contrasted with sunshine and friendliness. |
| | | | Allegretto ♩ = 100, light and nimble. |
| | | | Allegro ♩. = 112, sparkling and joyful; at times graceful and teasing. |
| | | | Allegro assai ♩ = 168, brilliant, demanding great sweep. |
| | Sonata No. 4 in E Minor (Köchel No. 304) | B 2 | Allegro ♩ = 94. The opening theme is caressing and kind; passages of make-believe gruffness. Passages of sparkling 8th notes and graceful melodies provide interesting contrast in this colorful movement. |

| COMPOSER | TITLE, KEY & OP. | GR. | REMARKS |
|---|---|---|---|
| Mozart, Wolfgang A. (Cont.) | Sonata No. 4 in E Minor (Köchel No. 304) | B 2 | Tempo di menuetto ♩ = 144, suggesting "happiness through tears." The E major section asks for caressing tenderness and affection. |
| | Sonata No. 5 in E-flat Major (Köchel No. 302) | B 2 | Allegro ♩ = 144-152, royal and festive; also expressive and affectionate. Brilliant passages and moments of wit and humor provide effective contrast. |
| | | | Rondo (Andante grazioso) ♩ = 94, distinguished and dignified; also sparkling and witty. |
| | Sonata No. 6 in G Major (Köchel No. 301) | B 2 | Allegro con spirito ♩ = 152. This movement begins with a theme of equisite beauty and bliss. It is soon contrasted by a passage of rhythmical decisiveness. Playful ideas follow. Brilliant passages in the piano part end the first section in flourish. A graceful second theme, followed by passages of great sweep is introduced, giving expression to exuberant joyfulness. The section after the double bar expresses rhythmical strength and playfulness. Sweeping passages in the piano follow and lead by way of graceful ideas back to the first theme. |
| | | | Allegro ♩ = 92. Its decisive rhythm expresses joy and happiness. The minore brings a note of wistfulness |
| | Sonata No. 7 in F Major (Köchel No. 376) | B 2 | Allegro ♩ = 144. Sweeping grandeur and a spirit of great joy characterize this movement. |
| | | | Andante ♩ = 52, affectionate and warmhearted. |

| Mozart, Wolfgang A. (Cont.) | Sonata No. 7 in F Major (Köchel No. 376) (Cont.) | B 2 | Rondo (Allegretto grazioso) ♩= 78, graceful, witty, sparkling and happy. |
|---|---|---|---|
| | Sonata No. 8 in C Major (Köchel No. 296) | B 2 | Allegro vivace ♩= 132, happy and alive. |
| | | | Andante sostenuto ♩= 54, mellow and warm, but also dreamy. The section after the double bar is rich and full. |
| | | | Rondo (Allegro ♩ = 112), happy; breathing joy of living. |
| | Sonata No. 9 in F Major (Köchel No. 377) | B 2 | Allegro ♩= 168, conveying a spirit of sweep and grandeur. |
| | | | Tema (Andante ♪= 100-104), wooing and tender. Vars. 1 and 2, the same as before. Var. 3, alive and florid. Var. 4, stately. Var. 5, expresses great simplicity. Var. 6, light-footed and graceful. |
| | | | Tempo di menuetto, un poco allegretto ♩= 104, unassuming and innocent. The section before the double bar is self-confident and warm. |
| | Sonata No. 10 in B-flat Major (Köchel No. 378) | B 2 | Allegro moderato ♩= 118, amiable and friendly; later brilliant. The wistful section after the double bar gives way to a section of dramatic fervor. |
| | | | Andantino sostenuto e cantabile ♩ = 52, mellow and tenderhearted. The section after the second double bar is rich and full. The end of the movement is of sublime beauty. |
| | | | Rondo (Allegro)♩.= 84, exuberantly happy and (Cont.) |

| COMPOSER | TITLE, KEY & OP. | GR. | REMARKS |
|---|---|---|---|
| Mozart, Wolfgang A. (Cont.) | Sonata No. 10 in B-flat Major (Köchel No. 378) (Cont.) | B 2 | joyful. The short allegro (♩=132) after the fermata, should be wide-awake and agile. |
| | Sonata No. 11 in G Major (Köchel No. 379) | B 2 | Adagio ♪ = 63-69, stately but expressive.<br><br>Allegro♩ =144, restless and anxious. After the second fermata, self-assured and brilliant.<br><br>Andantino cantabile♩ = 76-80. The theme is of charming simplicity. Var. 1, graceful and suave. Var. 2, playful. Var. 3, of sweeping grandeur. Var. 4, stern and serious. Var. 5, Adagio ♪=69, amiable and singing. The section after the double bar is stern.<br><br>Allegretto♩ = 92, suggesting a graceful swing. |
| | Sonata No. 12 in E-flat (Köchel No. 380) | B 2 | Allegro ♩= 126. The opening suggests authority and strength. Florid passage in triplets of light-footed grace provide for contrast. There are many moments of wit and sparkle in this wide-awake movement.<br><br>Andante con moto♩ = 60. The opening expresses pleading tenderness. After the double bar follow passages of great rhythmical vitality.<br><br>Rondo (Allegro)♩.= 100, gay and happy. |
| | Sonata No. 13 in A Major (Kochel No. 402) | B 2 | Andante ma un poco adagio ♩ = 69, dignified and aristocratic.<br><br>Allegro moderato♩ = 145, serious and severe. |

**Mozart, Wolfgang A. (Cont.)** — Sonata No. 14 in B-flat Major (Köchel No. 570)  **B 3**  Allegro ♩ = 176, amiable and graceful.

Adagio ♪ = 120, simple like a folk song, but not without affection. After the second double bar follows a section of imploring fervor.

Allegretto ♩ = 132, witty and sparkling.

Sonata No. 15 in B-flat Major (Köchel No. 454)  **B 3**  Largo ♪ = 80. The opening is majestic, soon giving way to tender thoughts.

Allegro ♩ = 152, happy and sunny; also brilliant and dashing.

Andante ♩ = 58, great emotional depth; warm and affectionate.

Allegretto ♩ = 88, joyful and happy; sometimes exuberantly so, sometimes in a more quiet way.

Sonata No. 16 in B-flat Major (Köchel No. 481)  **B 2**  Allegro molto ♩ = 176, happy and laughing; at times brilliant, but also imploringly tender.

Adagio ♩ = 76, affectionate and kind.

Tema (Allegretto) ♩ = 110, jovial and gay.

Var. 1, sunny and happy. Var. 2, playful and easy flowing. Var. 3, blunt and buffoonish. Var. 4, stern, but at times playful. Var. 5, naughty, sometimes boisterous. Var. 6, lightfooted and nimble.

Sonata No. 17 in A Major (Köchel No. 526)  **B 2**  Molto allegro ♩. = 110, exuberantly happy.

| COMPOSER | TITLE, KEY & OP. | GR. | REMARKS |
|---|---|---|---|
| Mozart, Wolfgang A. (Cont.) | Sonata No. 17 in A Major (Köchel No. 526) (Cont.) | B 2 | Andante ♩ = 60, dignified and serious; at times warmhearted.<br><br>Presto ♩ = 118, easy flowing; also brilliant and at times playful. |
| | Sonata No. 18 in F Major (Köchel No. 547) | B 2 | Andante cantabile ♩ = 94. The opening is simple like a folk song. The second and third section up to the recapitulation suggest more fervor. The section in B-flat major demands rhythmical decision.<br><br>Allegro ♩ = 138. The proud opening soon changes to a mood of persuasiveness. Brilliant passages and some graceful passages provide refreshing contrast.<br><br>Andante con variazioni ♩ = 76. The theme is of great simplicity. Var. 1, the same. Var. 2, rhythmically more pronounced. Var. 3, witty and gay. Var. 4, singing and smooth. Var. 5, warmhearted. Var. 6, brilliant. |
| | Concerto No. 3 in G Major (Köchel No. 216) | C 2 | Allegro ♩ = 120. The opening is festive and jubilant, giving way to affection and kindness. The grazioso suggests wit and fun. It is a movement of elusive inflections and of great charm. |
| | (cadenza by Joseph Szigeti) | | Adagio ♪ = 63. The opening suggests contentment and serene happiness, giving way to phrases of warmth and affection. The triplets in the accompaniment lend a special charm to this singing movement.<br><br>Allegro ♩. = 88, happy and light-footed. Pointed rhythm, vivacious 16th (Cont.) |

| COMPOSER | TITLE, KEY & OP. | GR. | REMARKS |
|---|---|---|---|
| Mozart, Wolfgang A. (Cont.) | Concerto No. 3 in G Major (Kochel No. 216) (Cont.) | C 2 | passages, and playful dialogues lend the background to this graceful movement. The charming andante ♩ = 63 and the spirited allegretto ♩ = 82 provide a delightful contrast. |
| | Concerto No. 4 in D Major (Joachim and Auer) | C 3 | Allegro ♪ = 132, royal and festive, at times playful and affectionate; almost always happy. |
| | (also cadenzas by Menuhin and Heifetz) | | Andante cantabile ♩ = 60, reflecting sublime happiness and contentment. A singing and graceful movement. |
| | | | Rondo (Andante grazioso) ♪ = 127, light, graceful and courteous. The Allegro non troppo ♩. = 96 is happy and gay. The Andante grazioso in G major ♩ = 58 is tender and affectionate. |
| | Concerto No. 5 in A Major (Joachim and Auer) | C 3 | Allegro aperto ♩ = 132. After the joyful tutti the solo violin starts the Adagio ♪ = 65, like a voice from heaven, pure and serene. The allegro aperto of the violin reflects sunshine and happiness; also warmth and affection. |
| | | | Adagio ♪ = 60, tender and affectionate. |
| | | | Tempo di menuetto ♩ = 112, graceful and charming. |
| | | | Allegro ♩ = 132, dashing, witty and brilliant. |
| | Concerto No. 6 in E-flat Major (Spiering) (Köchel No. 268) | C 3 | Allegro moderato ♩ = 120, royal and exalted; but also affectionate, sunny and playful. The C minor section of the second solo entrance changes to a serious but nevertheless warm and affectionate mood. The sublime phrase before the tutti |

| COMPOSER | TITLE, KEY & OP. | GR. | REMARKS |
|---|---|---|---|
| Mozart, Wolfgang, A. (Cont.) | Concerto No. 6 in E-flat Major (Spiering) (Köchel No. 268) (Cont.) | C 3 | which leads back to the opening idea, is one of the many high lights of the movement. |
| | | | Un poco adagio ♪ = 80, lofty and serene. A movement of pristine purity and of childlike innocence, but also of comforting warmth. |
| | | | Rondo (Allegretto) ♩ = 118, playful, happy and carefree; at times tender and affectionate. |
| Nardini, Pietro | Sonata in D Major (David) | C 2 | Adagio ♪ = 66, warm and affectionate. |
| | | | Allegro con fuoco ♩ = 132, proud and dashing; also playful, singing and affectionate. |
| | | | Larghetto - ♩ = 56, singing and affectionate. |
| | | | Allegretto ♩ = 88, happy and graceful. |
| | Concerto in E Minor (Sam Franko) | C 2 | Allegro moderato ♩ = 98, stately and dignified; at times singing and expressive. |
| | | | Andante cantabile ♩ = 86, a song of affection and tenderness. |
| | | | Allegretto giocoso ♩. = 84, joyful and spirited. |
| Nováček, Ottakar | Perpetuum mobile | C 2 | An excellent study in spiccato bowing. Also a very effective concert piece, full of color and contrasts. |
| Offenbach, Jacques | Barcarolle, from Les Contes d'Hoffmann, (Lilienthal) | A 2 | Singing and expressive, for pupils only. |
| Paganini, Nicolò | Moto perpetuo | C 3 | Featuring rapid 16th spiccato passages. |
| | La Campanella, Op. 7 | C 3 | See under Kreisler. |

| Paganini, Nicolò | Theme and Variations, "Non più mesta" Op. 12 | C 3 | Featuring expressive singing, spiccato, flying staccato, harmonics, left-hand pizzicati, runs in octaves, brilliant passages, etc. |
|---|---|---|---|
| | Theme and Variations, "Di Tanti Palpiti," Op. 13 (Kreisler) | C 3 | A charming theme with variations demanding a technic of the first rank. |
| | Witch's Dance (Le Streghe) | C 3 | The solo opens with a tender and affectionate cantilena inviting to rubato playing. The "Andantino leggiero" theme which follows becomes the basis for variations, displaying almost every witchery of the violin. |
| | Twenty-four caprices, Op. 1 (Becker) | C 3 | |
| | Caprice No. 1, Andante | | A study in arpeggios(bouncing bow). |
| | Caprice No. 2, Moderato | | A study in stretches of left hand and for string crossings. |
| | Caprice No. 3, Sostenuto   Presto | | A study in fingered octaves. A study for string crossings in legato passages. |
| | Caprice No. 4, Maestoso | | Study in double-stops. |
| | Caprice No. 5, Agitato | | Featuring brilliant scales and flying staccato. |
| | Caprice No. 6, Adagio | | A sustained melody with tremolando accompaniment. |
| | Caprice No. 7 | | A study in octaves, sustained chords, and fast staccato runs (firm staccato). |
| | Caprice No. 8, Maestoso | | A study for the development of the left hand. |

| COMPOSER | TITLE, KEY & OP. | GR. | REMARKS |
|---|---|---|---|
| Paganini, Nicolò (Cont.) | Caprice No. 9, Allegretto (arranged for concert by J. Thibaud) | | The first section imitates a flute and a horn in themes of decided rhythm. The middle section features ricochet bowing. |
| | Caprice No. 10, Vivace | | A study in flying staccato (martellato) and trills. |
| | Caprice No. 11, Andante | | A study in sustained chords. |
| | Presto | | A study in agile and dashing string crossings. |
| | Caprice No. 12, Allegro | | A study in even and smooth string crossings (Legato). |
| | Caprice No. 13, Allegro | | An excellent number for concert use. The opening is flexible and persuasive. The middle section features brilliant passages of trills and string crossings. |
| | Caprice No. 14, Moderato | | Study in double-stops. |
| | Caprice No. 15, Posato | | Featuring octaves and brilliant staccato runs. |
| | Caprice No. 16, Presto | | A study in accents and fast string crossings. |
| | Caprice No. 17, Sostenuto, Andante | | A study in fast scales and octave passages. |
| | Caprice No. 18, Corrente | | A study on the G string, suggesting bugle calls. |
| | Allegro | | Featuring agile double-stop scales in thirds. |
| | Caprice No. 19, Lento, Allegro assai | | A study in flying up-bow staccato and in heavy down-bow staccato. The middle section features passages on the G string. |
| | Caprice No. 20, Allegretto (Kreisler) | | Excellent concert number. The first section is singing and persuasive. The second part is brilliant and dashing. |

Paganini, Nicolò
(Cont.)

Twenty-four caprices
(Cont.)

Caprice No. 21,
Amoroso — Study in sixths, expressive and sentimental.

Presto — A brilliant study in fast staccato passages.

Caprice No. 22
Marcato — A study in sixths, thirds and tenths.

Minore — Featuring flying staccato passages and brilliant trills.

Caprice No. 23,
Posato — Study in octave glissandos.

Minore — Study in brilliant scale figures.

Caprice No. 24,
Tema (Quasi Presto)
and variations — A famous piece, also arranged for the piano. The tema is proud and decisive; variations of contrasting character follow.

Concerto in D Major,   C 3
Op. 6, No. 1
(cadenza by Emil
Sauret)

Allegro maestoso $\downarrow$ = 92. The opening is challenging and authoritative. A persuasive theme follows, but soon gives way to brilliant passages in thirds and to the return of the opening idea. A distinguished theme in C major leads to further display of brilliancy. This interchange of lyric ideas and dashing show of virtuosity gives to the soloist full opportunity to display the technical side as well as the singing character of the violin.

Adagio espressivo $\downarrow$ = 66. Intense fervor, imploring persuasiveness, moments of great dramatic power, imaginative rubato figurations, and the friendly theme in D major lend the background to this colorful movement.

Rondo (Allegro spirituoso) $\downarrow$ = 120, a sparkling, witty and dashing movement throughout.

| COMPOSER | TITLE, KEY & OP. | GR. | REMARKS |
|---|---|---|---|
| Persinger, Louis | Cancion del olvido (Spanish song) (Serrando) | C 2 | Singing. |
| | In the Time of Roses (Reichard) | C 2 | Unassuming and tender; some double-stops. |
| | Neapolitan Song (Barthemy) | C 1 | Warm and singing. |
| Pierne, Gabriel | Serenade in A | B 3 | Mostly for students. A light and graceful piece. |
| Popper, David | Gavotte in D No. 2, Op. 23 (Auer) | B 3 | Featuring flying staccato. |
| Prokofieff, Serge | Gavotte, Op. 32 (Heifetz) | C 2 | See under Heifetz. |
| | Larghetto and gavotte, from "Classical Sympnony," Op. 25 (Heifetz) | C 1 | Larghetto, graceful, dainty and distinguished. Gavotte, witty and humorous. |
| | Theme and processional from "Peter and the Wolf" (Grunes) | C 1 | Andantino, gently and expressive. Moderato, gay and swaggering. |
| | Kifé's wedding, from "Lieutenant Kijé" | C 1 | Graceful and gay; also moments of dolefulness and "wine happy" sentimentality. |
| | Three pieces, from "Romeo and Juliet" (Grunes) | C 1 | 1. Montaigus et Capulets: Allegro pesante, stately with grandeur. Moderato tranquillo, graceful and expressive. 2. Danse des jeunes Antillaises (Andante con eleganza), refined and graceful. 3. Masques (Andante marciale), clownish and humorous. |
| | March, from The Love for Three Oranges | C 2 | Witty, humorous and severely rhythmical. |
| | Concerto No. 2 in G Minor, Op. 63 | C 3 | Allegro moderato ♩ = 108. The opening is noble and dignified. The poco più mosso ♩ = 120, is playful |

- 68 -

(Cont.)

| COMPOSER | TITLE, KEY & OP. | GR. | REMARKS |
|---|---|---|---|
| Prokofieff, Serge (Cont.) | Concerto No. 2, in G Minor, Op. 63 (Cont.) | C 3 | and friendly. The meno mosso ♪.= 88, is romantic and affectionate. The più mosso ♪ = 132, is wild and tumultuous. After a brief dialogue in tempo 1, florid 16th passages lead to a bold and excited section having as a background the opening theme. After the lyric più tranquillo follows the più mosso, which starts in a hushed and mysteriously excited character. Relentlessly driving on, it leads through a broad climax back to the tempo initiale. The ideas of the first part are repeated and the tempo primo brings this noble movement to a dignified and satisfying end. |

Andante assai ♪= 112. This is a movement of great loftiness. The più animato ♪.= 58 is playful and easy flowing. The allegretto ♪ = 112 is sunny and happy.

Allegro ben marcato ♩ = 69-72. The opening theme is forceful and extremely rhythmical. A broad and nobly singing section follows. The 7/4 time is a playful episode of great rhythmical charm. The poco più mosso ♩.= 86 suggests intensive excitement. The tempo primo returns and the pattern of the first part is repeated in its main features. The fiery coda brings this virile and colorful movement to a tumultuous close.

| Rachmaninoff, Sergi | Hopak (Moussorgsky) | C 1 | Crisp and rhythmically decisive, featuring spiccato bowing. |

| COMPOSER | TITLE, KEY & OP. | GR. | REMARKS |
|---|---|---|---|
| Rachmaninoff, Sergi (Cont.) | Marguerite Album-leaf (Kreisler) | C 1 | Tenderly singing. |
| | Preghiera (Prayer from the piano concerto No. 2) (Kreisler) | C 1 | Affectionate and tender; building up to great fervor. |
| | Serenade (Elman) | C 2 | Affectionate and expressive. |
| Raff, J. | Cavatina Op. 85, No. 3, the same simplified (Ambrosio) | C 2 / A 2 | Broad and singing, also double stops. Mainly for pupils. |
| Rakov, Nicholas | Scherzino (Hartmann) | C 2 | Presto ♩ = 112, gay and spirited; featuring spiccato and ricochet bowing, also harmonics. |
| Rameau, J. P. | Passepied from the opera "Castor and Polux" (Szigeti) | C 1 | Allegretto, featuring light and flying staccato bowing. |
| Ravel, Maurice | Forlane from "le tombeau de Couperin" (Heifetz) | C 1 | Light and graceful, some double stops. |
| | Valses nobles et sentimentales Nos. 6 and 7 (Heifetz) | C 1 | No. 6, light and graceful. No. 7, smooth and imaginative. |
| | Piece en form de Habanera (Doney) | C 1 | Sensitive, imaginative, elusive and a little lazy. |
| | Pavane (Engel) | C 1 | Tenderly singing and expressive. |
| | Tzigane (Rhapsodie de concert) | C 3 | This colorful piece pictures in the "Lento quasi Cadenza" an improvising gypsy fiddler and calls for great imagination. The moderato ♪ = 88, suggests tantalizing restraint and pointed rhythm, but later on it becomes poignantly expressive. The meno vivo, grandioso ♩ = 76, expresses strutting pompousness and invites to rubato playing. Brilliant Cadenzas and dashing lively sections provide for contrast. The end of the (Cont.) |

| COMPOSER | TITLE, KEY & OP. | GR. | REMARKS |
|---|---|---|---|
| Ravel, Maurice (Cont.) | Tzigane (Rhapsodie de concert) (Cont.) | C 3 | piece builds up to a climax of wild frenzy. |
| Rehfeld, Fabian | Spanish dance Op. 47 No. 5 | C 1 | A short and graceful piece for the studio; featuring saltato and spiccato bowing. |
| | Spanish dance Op. 58 No. 1 | C 2 | Featuring left hand pizzicato and double stops. A spirited piece. Rubato and lazy sections provide a welcome contrast. |
| Rimsky-Korsakov, Nikolas | Song of India (Deery) from the opera "Sadko" (Kreisler) | B 2 / C 2 | Deery transcription for pupils only. / A sensitive and imaginative concert piece. |
| | Dance Orientale (Kreisler) | C 2 | Capricious and rhythmically crisp. |
| | Dance Arabe from "Scheherazade" (Kreisler) | C 2 | Easy flowing, sometimes happy, sometimes sad. |
| | Romance (Hartmann) | C 1 | Andantino espressivo; sustained and singing. |
| Rubinstein, Anton | Melodie in F Op. 3 also simplified by Ambrosio | B 1 / A 1 | Featuring sustained and singing tone. Mostly for pupils. |
| | Rêve angelique from "Komenoi Ostrow" Op. 10, No. 22 (Fanko) | B 3 | Sustained and singing; also double stops. For pupils only. |
| | Romance in E flat Major Op. 44 No. 1 (Hermann) | C 1 | Expressive and affectionate, building up to great emotional fervor. |
| Saint-Saëns, Camille | Swan (Le Cygne) Simplified by Ambrosio | B 1 / A 1 | Serene and descriptive; featuring a sustained legato. |
| | Havanaise Op. 83 | C 3 | Allegretto lusinghiero ♪ = 86, suggesting a Spanish atmosphere of comfortable indolence. Allegro ♩ = 160, brilliant and dashing. The following tempo primo has great charm and invites to rubato playing, providing also |

| COMPOSER | TITLE, KEY & OP. | GR. | REMARKS |
| --- | --- | --- | --- |
| Saint-Saëns, Camille (Cont.) | Havanaise Op. 83 (Cont.) | C 3 | sections of broad singing and playfulness. |
| | | | Allegro non troppo ♩ = 126, featuring brilliant glissando scales and builds up to a big climax. The final allegretto ♪ = 82 suggests a character of light hearted happiness. |
| | Introduction and Rondo Capriccioso, Op. 28 | C 3 | Andante malinconia ♩ = 52, wistful and tender. A florid cadenzalike passage leads to the |
| | | | Allegro ma non troppo ♩. = 88-92, capricious and tantalizing. There are moments of great poetry and passages of great brilliancy. In short, a piece of changing moods. |
| | Concerto No. 3 in B Minor, Op. 61 | C 3 | Allegro non troppo ♩ = 86. The opening is pompous and stately. The themes in B major and F-sharp major express poetry and imagination. |
| | | | Andantino quasi allegretto ♩. = 44. This movement is decidedly pastoral in character. The middle section builds up to a climax of sweeping grandeur. A cadenza-like improvisation (molto moderato) leads into the |
| | | | Allegro non troppo ♩ = 96. Iron-clad rhythm and flashy brilliancy characterize the opening theme of this movement. The theme in the G major section expresses angelic serenity. |
| Sarasate, Pablo | Caprice Basque, Op. 24 | C 2 | Moderato ♩ = 138, swaggering, but rhythmically clean cut. |
| | | | Allegro moderato ♩. = 104, sparkling, crisp and tantalizingly playful. |

| COMPOSER | TITLE, KEY & OP. | GR. | REMARKS |
| --- | --- | --- | --- |
| Sarasate, Pablo (Cont.) | Introduction et Tarantelle, Op. 43 | C 2 | Moderato ♩ = 88, affectionate and singing.<br><br>Allegro vivace ♩. = 192, sparkling and brilliant. |
| | Romanza Andaluza | C 2 | Warm and expressive; also sections of passion and sweep ♪· = 70. |
| | Spanish dances: | | |
| | Malagueña | C 2 | Andantino ♩. = 52, suave and mellow, at times playful and graceful. |
| | Habanera | C 3 | Allegretto ♩. = 104. Proud rhythm, brilliant scales, wistful moments and a scintilating coda lend the background to this charming piece. |
| | Zapadeato | C 3 | Featuring spiccato bowing in fast 6/8 rhythm ♩. = 132. |
| | Zigeunerweisen (Gypsy airs), Op. 20 | C 3 | Moderato ♪ = 58, an improvisation, featuring fiery passion, despairing melancholy and tender persuasion.<br><br>Un peu plus lent ♩ = 46, expressing wistful longing.<br><br>Allegro molto vivace ♩ = 160, signaling an outburst of wild joy. |
| Scarlatti, Domenico | Sonatina in D Major (Heifetz) | B 2 | Allegro ♩. = 96-104, a short piece in one movement, happy and gay; featuring spiccato bowing and double stops. For concert and studio. |
| | Twelve selected pieces (transcribed by J. Heifetz) | C 1 | Vol. 1<br>Andante from Suite No. 7, ♪ = 96, warm and affectionate but easy flowing.<br><br>Allegro from Suite No. 19, ♪ = 132, lively and gay. |

| COMPOSER | TITLE, KEY & OP. | GR. | REMARKS |
|---|---|---|---|
| Scarlatti, Domenico (Cont.) | Twelve selected pieces (transcribed by J. Heifetz) (Cont.) | C 1 | Minuetto (Moderato) ♩ = 138, light and graceful. |
| | | | Allegro from Suite No. 21 ♩ = 144, spirited and gay. |
| | | | Andante cantabile from Suite No. 38 ♩ = 100, singing and expressive. |
| | | | Allegro from Suite No. 38 ♩ = 132, spirited and lively. |
| | | | Vol. 2 |
| | | | Molto moderato ♩ = 96, from Suite No. 71 suggesting poise and dignity. |
| | | | Allegro from Suite No. 74 ♩ = 112, playful and gay. |
| | | | Presto from Suite No. 77 ♩. = 72, sparkling, spirited and gay. |
| | | | Pastorale from Suite No. 88, (Allegro) ♩. = 69 , easy flowing and graceful. |
| | | | Non presto (ma a tempo di ballo) ♩. = 84, gay, with decisive rhythm. |
| | | | Fuga from Suite No. 100 (Moderato) ♩. = 120, demanding sweep and vitality. |
| Schubert, Franz | Serenade ("Through the Leaves") | A 2 | Graceful and singing; also affectionate and warm. |
| | Simplified by Ambrosio | A 1 | |
| | Ave Maria (Wilhelmj) (Heifetz) | C 2 | Sustained and singing; also double-stops. |
| | Simplified | B 2 | |
| | Moment Musical No. 3 (Kreisler) | C 1 | See under Kreisler. |

| COMPOSER | TITLE, KEY & OP. | GR. | REMARKS |
|---|---|---|---|
| Schubert, Franz | Rondo brilliant in B Minor, Op. 70 | C 3 | Andante ♩ = 56, stately and proud; at times tender and affectionate. |
| | | | Allegro ♩ = 125, sunny and sublimely happy; at times changing to a healthy gruffness. |
| | Three sonatinas, Op. 137 | B 3 | |
| | No. 1, in D Major | | Allegro molto ♩ = 112, friendly and easy flowing. |
| | | | Andante ♪ = 104, sunny and distinguished. The middle section is affectionate and warm. |
| | | | Allegro vivace ♪. = 108, amiable and playful; has moments of dramatic sweep. |
| | No. 2, in A Minor | | Allegro moderato ♩ = 114, singing, easy flowing and graceful; at times dramatic. |
| | | | Andante ♪ = 94, noble and eloquent. |
| | | | Menuetto (Allegro) ♩ = 138, serious and severe. The trio is affectionate and tender. |
| | | | Allegro ♩ = 134, wistful and tenderhearted; has moments of dramatic sweep. |
| | No. 3, in G Minor | | Allegro giusto ♩ = 120, a movement of great contrasts; challenging forcefulness giving way to imploring tenderness; dramatic moments changing to sunshine and happiness. |
| | | | Andante ♪ = 76, suggesting poise and dignity. The middle section changes to imploring fervor. |

| COMPOSER | TITLE, KEY & OP. | GR. | REMARKS |
|---|---|---|---|
| Schubert, Franz (Cont.) | No. 3, in G Minor (Cont.) | B 3 | Menuetto ♩= 132, happy and sunny. The trio is suave and graceful. |
| | | | Allegro moderato ♩= 112, affectionate and tender; has moments of sunny playfulness. |
| Schumann, Robert | Fantasy in C Major Op. 131 (Kreisler) | C 3 | Moderato ♩= 84, affectionate and imaginative, suggesting rubato playing. |
| | | | Allegro marcato e molto moderato ♩= 92, joyful and rhythmically decisive. The più tranquillo is tender and poetic. After the eloquent cadenza the movement builds up to a festive climax. |
| | Two sonatas for piano and violin: | | |
| | Sonata in A Minor, Op. 105 | C 2 | Mit leidenschaftlichem Ausdruck ♩.= 80. Smoldering passion, rhythmical strength, brilliant passages form the background to this stormy movement. |
| | | | Allegretto ♪= 96. The opening suggests the character of a fairy tale, a story of intimate and tender charm. The F minor section is poetic and sensitive; the bewegter suggests a picture of a mischievous kobold. |
| | | | Lebhaft ♩= 116, sparkling and crisp; at times warm and passionate. |
| | Sonata in D Minor, Op. 121 | C 2 | Ziemlich langsam ♩= 63, rhythmically decisive; at times imaginative and tenderly expressive. |
| | | | Lebhafter ♩= 120, dramatic and fervently passionate. |

| COMPOSER | TITLE, KEY & OP. | GR. | REMARKS |
|---|---|---|---|
| Schumann, Robert (Cont.) | Sonata in D Minor, Op. 121 (Cont.) | C 2 | Sehr lebhaft ♩.= 120, rhythmically crisp and decisive. The F-sharp minor section is tenderly wooing. |
| | | | Leise, einfach ♪ = 84, soft and unassuming; etwas bewegter is stormy. |
| | | | Bewegt ♪= 118, passionate and fiery. |
| Scott, Cyril | Lotus Land, Op. 47, No. 1 (Kreisler) | C 1 | Andante languido, exotic and colorful. The opening is sensitive and imaginative, building up to dramatic fervor. |
| | Danse nègre, Op. 58, No. 5 (W. Kramer) | C 1 | Molto vivace, spirited and and playful. |
| | Irish lament | C 1 | Moderato, sustained and and expressive (sordino). |
| Seitz, Fr. | Pupil concertos: | | |
| | No. 1, in D Major (first to seventh position) | C 2 | These concertos are for pupils only. They offer splendid material for the development of the left hand and a well-balanced bow technic. They are stimulating musically and give the student an appreciation of singing tone, also for musicianship. Nos. 2 and 5 are the easiest. Nos. 3 and 4 are for more advanced students. No. 1 is quite difficult. |
| | No. 2, in G Major, Op. 13 (first position) | A 2 | |
| | No. 3, in G Minor, Op. 12 (first to third position) | B 3 | |
| | No. 4, in D Major, Op. 15 (first to third position) | B 3 | |
| | No. 5, in D Major, Op. 22 (first position) | A 2 | |
| Shostakovich, Dmitri | Three fantastic dances, Op. 1 (H. Glickman) | | |
| | 1. Allegretto | C 2 | Graceful and imaginative. |
| | 2. Andantino | C 2 | Somewhat lazy. |
| | 3. Allegretto | C 2 | Light and humorous. |

| COMPOSER | TITLE, KEY & OP. | GR. | REMARKS |
|---|---|---|---|
| Shostakovich, Dmitri (Cont.) | Polka, from the "Golden Age"(ballet), Op. 22 (H. Glickman) | C 1 | Humorous, witty and burlesque, featuring spiccato bowing. |
| | Satirical dance, from "The Bolt" (polka) (R. Forst) | C 2 | Clownish, burlesque, pompous and whimisical. A piece of spirit and contrasts. |
| | Four preludes (Tziganov-Maganini) | C 2 | 1. <u>Moderato</u> <u>non</u> <u>troppo</u>, wistful and graceful. |
| | | | 2. <u>Allegretto</u>, gay and sparkling. |
| | | | 3. <u>Andantino</u>, rhythmically decisive. |
| | | | 4. <u>Allegretto</u>, satiric. |
| Sibelius, Jean | Valse Triste (Franko) | C 1 | An extremely sad piece based on a drama by Jarnefeld entitled "Kuolema" (death). |
| | Romance, Op. 24, No. 9 | C 1 | Singing and full. |
| | Concerto in D Minor, Op. 47 | C 3 | <u>Allegro</u> <u>moderato</u> $\quartnote$ = 69-72. The opening suggests a mood of poetic trance, changing soon to intense passion. Sweeping passages and a rubato <u>largamente</u> follow. The <u>molto moderato</u> $\quartnote$ = 46 is poetic and affectionate. It builds up to great warmth and fervor. After subsiding to a dreamy fermata, the mood changes and leads to the forceful <u>allegro</u> <u>molto</u> $\quartnote$ = 138. An imaginative cadenza follows, the pattern of the first part is repeated, and the movement ends on a note of exuberant triumph. |
| | | | <u>Adagio</u> <u>di</u> <u>molto</u> $\eighthnote$ = 72, warm, serious and eloquent; demanding great emotional depth. |

| COMPOSER | TITLE, KEY & OP. | GR. | REMARKS |
|---|---|---|---|
| Sibelius, Jean (Cont.) | Concerto in D Minor, Op. 47 (Cont.) | C 3 | Allegro ma non tanto ♩ = 100. Uncompromisingly severe rhythm, sweeping grandeur, and playful syncopations give the main character to this intense and virile movement. |
| Sinding, Christian | Romance in E Minor. Op. 10 (Svečenski) | C 2 | Presto, featuring fast 16th passages. A moto perpetuo.<br><br>Adagio, eloquent and dignified.<br><br>Tempo giusto, suggesting great breadth and authority. |
| Sitt, Hans | Student Concerto No. 1 in C Major, Op. 104 (first position) | A 3 | These concertos furnish excellent teaching material for the development of the left hand and the bow arm. They also provide for the student the fundamentals of style and musicianship. |
| | Concertino in E Minor, Op. 31 (first to third position) | A 3 | |
| | Students' concertino No. 2 in A Minor, Op. 108 (first to third position) | B 3 | |
| | Concertino No. 3 in D Minor, Op. 110 (first to fifth position) | C 1 | |
| | Concertino in D Minor, Op. 65 (first to fifth position) | C 1 | |
| Spalding, Albert | Gavotte-Pompadour | B 2 | Tempo di Gavotte, light and gay. Molto tranquillo, quiet and gentle. |
| | Lettre de Chopin | C 1 | Tempo di mazurka, graceful, caressing and suave. |
| | Ballhausplatz | C 1 | Affectionate and graceful. |

| COMPOSER | TITLE, KEY & OP. | GR. | REMARKS |
|---|---|---|---|
| Spalding, Albert (Cont.) | Old Irish song and dance based on "Norah O'Neill and Foggy dew" | C 1 | Simple and flowing, in the character of a folk song.<br><br>Gay and lively, in the character of a folk dance. |
| | Castles in Spain Op. 7, No. 4 | C 2 | Featuring spiccato, ricochet bowing, and harmonics. |
| | Dragon fly (Study in Arpeggios) | C 2 | Allegretto, featuring fast ricochet figurations. |
| | Wind in the pines | C 2 | Moderato, imaginative and colorful. |
| | Hark, hark the lark (Schubert) | C 2 | Light and graceful, with an easy sway. |
| | Rondo brilliant (La Gaite), Op. 62 (Weber) | C 2 | Nimble and graceful; also dashing and brilliant. |
| Spohr, Louis | Concerto No. 7 in E Minor, Op. 38 | C 3 | Allegro ♩ = 106, featuring brilliant and flashy passage work; also melodies of ardent warmth.<br><br>Adagio ♪ = 104-108, mellow and singing; has sections of dramatic fervor, inviting to rubato playing.<br><br>Rondo ♪ = 168, graceful, courteous and elegant. |
| | Concerto No. 8 in A in form of a vocal scene, Op. 47 | C 3 | Allegro molto ♩ = 144. After a short tutti, the solo violin enters with a recitativo in the style of a lyric scene in an Italian opera. The adagio in F major ♪ = 72 calls for a tone of pure gold to do full justice to its poetic beauty. The A-flat section becomes more animated, even highly dramatic.<br><br>The Andante ♩ = 72, somewhat like a recitative, leads to the allegro moderato ♩ = 114. A brilliant movement, featuring trills and staccato runs. |

| COMPOSER | TITLE, KEY & OP. | GR. | REMARKS |
|---|---|---|---|
| Spohr, Louis (Cont.) | Concerto No. 8 in A in form of a vocal scene, Op. 47 (Cont.) | | It may be debatable whether the concertos by Spohr should still be played in public; but there can be no doubt that the Concerto No. 8 and the 2nd and 3rd movements of No. 7 are gems of rare beauty which should be included in our present-day programs. As teaching material all of them are still of great value. |
| Stoessel, Albert | Minuet on a theme by Tchaikovsky | B 3 | Amiable and graceful. Mostly for studio use. |
| | March Orientale | B 1 | Allegro. For studio use. |
| | Lullaby, Op. 8, No. 1 | B 2 | Andante (con sordino), some double-stops. For studio. |
| | Humoresque, Op. 8, No. 2 | B 3 | Allegretto, light and gay, featuring spiccato bowing and double-stops. For studio. |
| | Falling Leaves | C 1 | Andante, expressive and tender, has moments of passionate fervor. |
| | Crinoline, minuet in olden style | B 3 | Graceful and quaint; featuring double-stops, spiccato and pizzicato. For studio. |
| | Aladdin | B 2 | Presto, a short and light piece 5/8 time. For studio. |
| | Ariette | A 2 | Andante, expressive and singing. For studio. |
| Stoeving, Paul | Capriccio Rustico | C 1 | Vivace ma non troppo, gay and spirited. The più lento is graceful and tender. Features ricochet and spiccato bowing. For studio. |
| Stone, Gregory | Hora Burlesca | C 2 | Allegro giocoso e ben ritmato, gay and spirited. |
| | Doina (a romantic caprice) | C 2 | Andante; alla Zingera e rubato molto, free, in the style of an improvising gypsy. |

| COMPOSER | TITLE, KEY & OP. | GR. | REMARKS |
|---|---|---|---|
| Stone, Gregory (Cont.) | Doina (a romantic caprice) (Cont.) | C 2 | Allegro vivo, fiery and gay. |
| | Hora spiccato | C 2 | Allegro brilliant, lively and gay. |
| | | | Andante capriccioso, doleful; has moments of fiery passion. |
| Strauss, Richard | Beside the Spring, Op. 9, No. 2 | B 2 | Poetic and dreamy, soft and singing. Mostly for studio use. |
| | Sonata in E-flat Major, Op. 18 | C 3 | Allegro ma non troppo ♩ = 100. The opening is stately and festive, changing soon to persuasive tenderness. Sections of passion and intense fervor follow. A romantic and colorful movement. |
| | | | Improvisation (Andante cantabile) ♪ = 69, highly poetic and romantic. The middle section is passionate and animated. |
| | | | Finale: Andante ♪ = 80, mysterious. |
| | | | Allegro ♩ = 116, challenging, brilliant and dashing; also sections of playfulness and romantic singing. |
| Suk, Joseph | Love Song, Op. 7, No. 1 (S. Harmati) | C 2 | Affectionate and warm. The middle section builds up to great fervor. |
| | Un poco triste, Op. 17, No. 3 | C 1 | Andante espressivo, singing and dolefully expressive. |
| | Burleska, Op. 17, No. 4 | C 2 | Allegro vivace, spirited and lively; featuring fast spiccato bowing. |
| Svendsen, Johan S. | Romance in G, Op. 26 | C 2 | Andante, singing and affectionate. Più mosso, restless and animated. |

| COMPOSER | TITLE, KEY & OP. | GR. | REMARKS |
|---|---|---|---|
| Szigeti, Joseph | Air Russe and Rondo, from the third sonata by Weber | C 2 | Allegro moderato, graceful and light. Rondo (Presto), fleeting but joyful. |
| | Pieds-en-l'air, from the "Capriol" Suite (Warlock) | C 2 | Andantino tranquillo, quietly singing. |
| | Three pieces, from the "Capriol" Suite (Warlock) | C 2 | 1. Basse-Dance: Allegro moderato, graceful but dignified. |
| | | | 2. Pavane: Allegretto un poco lento, graceful and gentle. All in double-stops. |
| | | | 3. Mattachius: Allegro con brio, gay and rhythmical; building up to a great climax at the close. |
| | Paganini Caprice No. 2 in B Minor | C 3 | Arranged for concert performance by Szigeti. |
| | Etude in thirds, Op. 8, No. 10 (Screabine) | C 2 | |
| | Snow (Norwegian Song) (Sigurd lie) | A 3 | Lento non troppo, soft and gentle; many harmonics. |
| Szymanowski, Karol | La fontaine d'Aréthuse Op. 30, No. 1 | C 2 | A slow, imaginative and colorful piece; has sections of passionate fervor. |
| | Chant de Roxane (Kochanski) | C 2 | Dreamy and poetic. |
| | Notturno and Tarantella Op. 28, Nos. 1 and 2 | C 2 | Notturno (Lento assai), poetic and dreamy. Allegretto scherzando is light and rhythmical. There are moments of passion and of tender affection. |
| | | | Tarantella (Presto appassionata), fiery and passionate, with a relentless drive, barely interrupted by the affectionate meno mosso. |

| COMPOSER | TITLE, KEY & OP. | GR. | REMARKS |
|---|---|---|---|
| Tartini, Guiseppe | Variations on a theme by Corelli (Kreisler) | C 2 | Allegro <u>ma</u> <u>non</u> <u>troppo</u> ♩ = 88. The theme is proud and stately. Vars. 1 and 2, sparkling. Var. 3, stately and authoritative. |
| | Devil's Trill (Kreisler) | C 2 | Larghetto ♪ = 112, persuasive, at times intensely emotional. |
| | | | Allegro <u>energico</u> ♩ = 90, challenging; also playful and humorous. |
| | | | Grave ♪ = 78, compelling and authoritative. |
| | | | Allegro <u>assai</u> ♩ = 138, teasing, at times sarcastic; then again persuasive. According to the legend, the devil was sitting one night at the foot of Tartini's bed playing for him the so-called "Devil's trill." As the name implies, trills are greatly featured in this piece. |
| | Sonata in G Minor (Auer) | B 3 | Adagio ♪ = 72, expressive and affectionate. |
| | | | Non <u>troppo</u> <u>presto</u> ♩ = 152, vigorous and rhythmical; also playful. |
| | | | Largo ♩ = 78, majestic; also tender and expressive. |
| | | | Allegro <u>commodo</u> ♩.= 72, easy flowing and graceful. |
| Tchaikovsky, Peter Ilich | Russian dance (B. Koutzen) | C 2 | A florid cadenza, a simple Russian folk song, followed by a gay and spirited <u>allegro vivo</u>. |
| | Valse sentimentale, Op. 51, No. 6 (M. Press) | C 1 | Wistful and tender. |
| | Romance (Swett-Centano) | B 3 | Andante <u>cantabile</u>, wistful, caressing and expres- (Cont.) |

- 84 -

| COMPOSER | TITLE, KEY & OP. | GR. | REMARKS |
|---|---|---|---|
| Tchaikovsky, Peter Ilích (Cont.) | Romance (Swett-Centano) (Cont.) | B 3 | sive. <u>Allegro energico</u>, vigorous and spirited. |
| | Dance of the Mirlitons, from "Nutcracker Suite" (Share and Zimbalist) | C 2 | Light and gay; featuring spiccato bowing, double-stops, harmonics and ricochets. |
| | Arabe dance, from "Nutcracker Suite" (Share and Zimbalist) | C 2 | Melancholy and doleful. Features double-stops and harmonics. |
| | Chinese dance, from "Nutcracker Suite" (Share and Zimbalist) | C 2 | Featuring fingered octaves, harmonics, and left-hand pizzicati. |
| | Humoresque (Hartmann) | B 3 | <u>Allegretto</u> scherzando, light and gay. The middle section is expressive and tender. |
| | Barcarolle Op. 37, No. 6 (Saenger) | B 2 | Wistful and tender. |
| | Air de Lensky ("O days of youth"), from <u>Eugen Onegin</u> | C 1 | Sustained and expressive. Features double-stops and florid cadenzas. |
| | Chanson sans paroles | B 1 | <u>Allegretto grazioso</u>, singing and graceful. For pupils. |
| | Andante from the string quartet, Op. 11 (Auer and Kreisler) | C 1 | See under Auer. |
| | Autumn Song, Op. 37, No. 10 | C 1 | See under Hartmann. |
| | Sérénade Mélancolique, in B-flat Minor, Op. 26 | C 1 | Sustained and sobbing. The <u>piu mosso</u> is free and flexible. The <u>largamente</u> is pompous. |
| | Valse, Op. 40, No. 8 | C 1 | Persuasive and suave. |
| | Mélodie, Op. 42, No. 3 | C 1 | Singing and expressive. The middle section is graceful and light. |
| | Concerto in D Major, Op. 35 | C 3 | <u>Allegro moderato</u> ♩ = 120, <u>Moderato assai</u> ♩ = 80, brilliant passage work alternates with themes of Slavic warmth and fervor. |

| COMPOSER | TITLE, KEY & OP. | GR. | REMARKS |
|---|---|---|---|
| Tchaikovsky, Peter Ilîch (Cont.) | Concerto in D Major, Op. 35 (Cont.) | C 3 | Andante (Canconetta) ♩ = 69. The first and third sections are wistful and melancholy. The middle section suggests hope and confidence. |
| | | | Allegro vivacissimo ♩ = 160, extremely rhythmical and brilliant. The molto meno mosso section expresses deep melancholy. |
| Thibaut, Jacques | La Chasse (caprice by Paganini) | C 3 | Allegretto, featuring double-stops and ricochet bowing. |
| | Minute Caprice (Rode) | C 2 | Presto, featuring fast 16th figurations in 3/8 time. |
| Thomé, Francis | Simple Aveu (romance) | B 2 | Moderato, sustained and singing. Used in church. |
| | Andante Religioso, Op. 70 | C 2 | Sustained and singing. |
| Veracini, Francesco, Maria | Concert sonata, Op. 2, No. 8 (Gustav Jensen) | B 3 | Allegro moderato ♩ = 112, spirited and gay. |
| | | | Ritornello (Largo) ♪ = 60, stately and dignified; at times tender and expressive. |
| | | | Giga (Allegro) ♩. = 116, suggesting vigor and sweep; also at times playfulness. |
| | Sonata in E Minor (F. David) | B 3 | Ritornello (Largo) ♪ = 72. After a stately and authoritative opening in the piano, the violin sings with warmth and fervor. |
| | | | Allegro con fuoco ♩ = 120, brilliant and spirited; at times playful and humorous. |
| | | | Menuet ♩ = 80, graceful and affectionate. |
| | | | Gavotte ♩ = 80, spirited and humorous. |
| | | | Presto ♩. = 132, lively and spirited. |

| COMPOSER | TITLE, KEY & OP. | GR. | REMARKS |
|---|---|---|---|
| Vieuxtemps, Henri | Rêverie, Op. 22, No. 3 | C 1 | Adagio, suggesting great pathos and intense fervor. |
| | Air varié, Op. 22, No. 2 | C 2 | Introduction (Andante), warm and expressive. |
| | | | Allegretto, easy flowing and friendly. Var. 1, graceful, at times brilliant. Var. 2, pompous and with rhythmical decision. Var. 3, featuring long staccato runs and other brilliant passages. (Mostly for studio.) |
| | Fantasia appassionata | C 3 | Allegro moderato, pompous. |
| | | | Andante, affectionate and warm; at times passionate. |
| | | | Moderato, friendly and charming. |
| | | | Largo, warm and affectionate. |
| | | | Finale (Allegro vivace), spirited and lively. |
| | Ballade and Polonaise, Op. 38 | C 2 | Ballade ♩ = 76, suggesting the telling of a fairy tale. |
| | | | Polonaise ♩ = 96, pompous and brilliant; has moments of lyric tenderness. |
| | Concerto No. 1 in E Major | C 3 | Musically the least important of his concertos; featuring long and fast staccato runs. |
| | Concerto No. 4 in D Minor, Op. 31 | C 3 | Andante ♩ = 80, pompous and passionate. The moderato ♩ = 84 is poetic and free; building up to a great climax before the brilliant cadenza. |
| | | | Adagio religioso ♩. = 54, exalted and pontifical; building up to climactic fervor. |

| COMPOSER | TITLE, KEY & OP. | GR. | REMARKS |
|---|---|---|---|
| Vieuxtemps, Henri (Cont.) | Concerto No. 4 in D Minor, Op. 31 (Cont.) | C 3 | Scherzo ♩. = 110, sparkling and witty. The meno mosso ♩. = 80 is eloquent and singing. |
| | | | Allegro ♩ = 80. The opening solo demands uncompromisingly severe rhythm. There follow sections of persuasion and tenderness. The end of the movement builds to a great climax. |
| | Concerto No. 5 in A Minor | C 3 | Allegro non troppo ♩ = 104 (at times a little slower). The opening solo is free and imaginative. The lyric sections are warm and affectionate, at times exalted and passionate. Dashing passages, featuring characteristic and intricate bowings provide for welcome contrast. The tempo throughout the movement is quite flexible. |
| | | | Adagio ♩ = 60-69, eloquent and expressive. There are also moments of innocent simplicity and fervent warmth. It is a movement of great contrasts. |
| | | | Allegro con fuoco ♩ = 112, a short and brilliant section, bringing the movement to a close. |
| Viotti, Giovanni Battista | Concerto No. 22 in A Minor (Joachim; also cadenza by Joachim) | C 2 | Moderato ♩ = 112. The solo opening is warm and mellow. Brilliant passages demanding expert trill and bow control, provide effective contrast to the lyric sections of the movement. |
| | | | Adagio ♪ = 74, a movement of great poetry and imagination. |
| | | | Agitato assai ♩ = 108. Severe rhythm and brilliant passages lend the background to this sparkling movement. |

| COMPOSER | TITLE, KEY & OP. | GR. | REMARKS |
|---|---|---|---|
| Viotti, Giovanni Battista (Cont.) | Concerto No. 22 in A Minor (Joachim; also cadenza by Joachim) (Cont.) | C 2 | This concerto was a favorite of Brahms. It is still held in high esteem by lovers of fine music. (Excellent teaching material.) |
| | Concerto No. 23 in G Major | B 2 | A concerto for studio use only. Excellent for developing style and technic. |
| Vitali, Tommaso | Ciacona in G Minor (Charlier-Auer) | C 2 | Theme and variations of widely different character, bringing into use many kinds of bowing. Besides being a fine concert piece, it represents excellent teaching material. |
| Vivaldi, Antonio | Concerto in G Minor (Nachez) | B 2 | Allegro ♩ = 88, stately but also playful; at times warm and expressive.

Adagio ♪ = 80, glowing and warm.

Allegro ♩. = 66, lively and gay; at times tenderly expressive. An excellent piece for style and bow technic. |
| | Concerto in A Minor, Op. 3, No. 6 (Nachez) | B 2 | Allegro, broad and dignified; also playful.

Largo, singing and warm.

Presto, gay and rhythmically alive; also playful. |
| | Sonata in D Major (Respighi) | C 1 | Moderato (A fantasia) ♩ = 50, in the character of an improvisation, requiring imagination and freedom.

Allegro moderato ♩ = 90, rhythmically severe, a movement of great vitality.

Largo ♩ = 48, a movement of great depth; requiring breadth and sustaining power of the bow. |

| COMPOSER | TITLE, KEY & OP. | GR. | REMARKS |
|---|---|---|---|
| Vivaldi, Antonio (Cont.) | Sonata in D Major (Respighi) (Cont.) | C 1 | Vivace ♩= 126, playful and and charming; at times exuberantly joyful. Requires great rhythmical control. |
| Wagenaar, Bernard | Sonata for violin and piano | C 2 | The first movement, in the classic sonata allegro form, begins with an introduction, in which the basic harmonic and melodic motive is introduced. The allegro proper opens with an undulating D major subject of lyrical sweep. The second subject, in E major, is of a quieter character. The development section, which follows, leads to a shortened return of the first subject, which prepares the recapitulation of the shortened second subject. A coda referring to the introductory chords ends the movement. |

The second movement is a scherzo in 7/4 time, composed as a "Song form with Trio," the latter being in 3/2 meter and of a passionate and melodic character; providing relief from the vivacious scherzo section.

The third movement is a romanza in the "three-part song form," a simple, melodic line, supported by warm and interesting harmonies.

The last movement is a lively and dashing sonata-allegro of approximately the same proportions as the first movement; thus serving as a suitable finale to a work in the larger forms of composition that is characteristic of recent times. It is rewarding and attractive in its frank romanticism.

| COMPOSER | TITLE, KEY & OP. | GR. | REMARKS |
|---|---|---|---|
| Wagner, Richard | Grand march, from Tannhäuser (simplified by Ambrosio) | A 2 | In the first position. |
| | Bridal march, from Lohengrin (Centano) | B 2 | Mostly first position. |
| | Song to the Evening Star | A 2 | Sustained and singing. |
| | Walter's Prize Song, from Meistersinger | B 3 | Good teaching material for tone. |
| | Also arranged by Wilhelmj | C 2 | |
| | Albumleaf (Romance) (Wilhelmj) | C 2 | Romantic, warm and singing. The middle section builds up to intense fervor. |
| | "Dreams", from the 5 poèmes (Auer) | C 2 | Sustained, affectionate and poetic. |
| Weber, Carl Maria von | Laendler (Willeke) | C 1 | See under Willeke. |
| | Larghetto (Kreisler) | C 2 | A short piece of an expressive but also graceful character. |
| | Country dance (Elman) | C 1 | Graceful and friendly; featuring flying staccato. |
| | Rondo from the piano sonata, Op. 24 (Press) | C 2 | Presto, a perpetuum mobile in fast 16th passages; mostly legato in character. |
| | Waltz No. 1 (Burmester) | B 3 | Graceful and friendly; featuring flying staccato. the trio is legato and wistful. |
| | Waltz No. 2 (Burmester) | B 3 | Gay and joyful; featuring flying staccato and double-stops. |
| Wieniawski, Henri | Légende, Op. 17 | C 2 | Andante moderato, expressive and wistful. |
| | Simplified by Ambrosio | A 2 | Allegro moderato, singing in double-stops. |
| | Caprice in E Major (Heifetz) | C 3 | Featuring flying staccato and double-stops. |

43257

| COMPOSER | TITLE, KEY & OP. | GR. | REMARKS |
|---|---|---|---|
| Wieniawski, Henri (Cont.) | Obertass, mazurka, Op. 29, No. 1 | C 2 | Featuring double-stops and decisive rhythm. For studio only. |
| | Simplified by Ambrosio | A 2 | |
| | Souvenir de Moscou | C 3 | See under Kreisler (Airs Russe). |
| | Capriccio Valse, Op. 7 (Auer) | C 2 | Allegretto, light, graceful and friendly. |
| | | | Presto, featuring long and rapid staccato runs. |
| | Scherzo Tarantelle, Op. 16 (Spiering) | C 2 | Presto, a fast and brilliant piece in 6/8 time. The G major and D major sections call for suave singing. |
| | Polonaise in D Major, Op. 4 | C 3 | Pompous and sweeping; sometimes graceful and persuasive; at other times brilliant and flashy. |
| | Polonaise in A Major, Op. 21 | C 3 | Brilliant, happy and graceful. Featuring long staccato passages (flying staccato). |
| | Concerto No. 1 in F-sharp Minor, Op. 14 (Auer) | C 3 | This concerto is technically one of the most difficult. Allegro moderato ♩ = 100, Moderato e maestoso ♩ = 92, pompous and challenging dashing and brilliant. |
| | | | Preghiera (Larghetto) ♩ = 70, sustained and broad; entirely on the G string. |
| | | | Rondo (Allegro giocoso) ♩ = 96, joyful, graceful and witty; the majore is warm and singing. |
| | Concerto No. 2 in D Minor, Op. 22 | C 3 | This is a most "violinistic" concerto. It makes full use of all the possibilities of the instrument and at the same time remains charming and delightful music. (Cont.) |

| COMPOSER | TITLE, KEY & OP. | GR. | REMARKS |
|---|---|---|---|
| Wieniawski, Henri (Cont.) | Concerto No. 2 in D Minor, Op. 22 (Cont.) | C 3 | Allegro moderato ♩ = 108. Melodies of sensuous tone beauty, brilliant passages, long staccato runs, glissandos, etc., provide the background for this very effective movement. |
| | | | Romance (Andante non troppo ♩.= 70, dreamy and poetic; at times intensely passionate. Always extremely singing. |
| | | | Allegro con fuoco ♩ = 144, a brilliant but free interlude, leading to the |
| | | | Allegro moderato (a la Zingara) ♩ = 138, a piece of outspoken gypsy character. Its sparkling spiccato passages, sensuous melodies, passionate climaxes, and wild yet decisive rhythm give it a character of irresistible briliancy. |
| Wilhelmj, August | Ave Maria (Schubert) | C 2 | See under Schubert. |
| | Romance in E Major, Op. 10 | C 2 | Singing and expressive. |
| | Swedish Melody (Vermeland) | C 1 | A short piece of a wistful character. |
| Willeke, Willem | Canzonetta | C 1 | Gay and spirited; the F major section is affectionate and singing. |
| | Chant sans paroles in A Major | C 1 | Moderato, singing. Some double stops. |
| | Rondo (Boccherini), from string quintet | C 2 | Gay and happy; at times affectionate. Featuring flying staccato. |
| | Laendler (Weber) | C 1 | Friendly and graceful. Featuring flying staccato. |

| COMPOSER | TITLE, KEY & OP. | GR. | REMARKS |
|----------|-----------------|-----|---------|
| Winn, E. L. | Five playtime pieces for little violinists | A 1 | For beginners. Start with open strings. They are short and stimulating. Verses help to keep the interest of these very young pupils. |
| Winternitz, Felix | The Blue Lagoon (Millöcker) | C 2 | <u>Moderato assai,</u> affectionate and singing; featuring double-stops throughout. |
| | Dream of Youth | C 2 | Tenderly expressive; featuring double-stops. |
| | Troika, capriccio | C 2 | Featuring light spiccato bowing. The <u>più tranquillo</u> is wistful and singing. |
| | Forsaken (Carinthian melody) (Koschat) | C 1 | <u>Andante</u>, singing and expressive. |
| Ysaye, Eugène | Sonatas for violin alone | C 3 | At present out of print. |
| Zimbalist, Efrem | Scherzo (Tchaikovsky) Op. 42, No. 2 | C 1 | <u>Presto giocoso</u>, featuring brilliant spiccato figures in 6/8 time. The middle section is expressive. |
| | Dance of the Mirlitons | C 2 | See under Tchaikovsky. |
| | Arabe dance | C 2 | ''      ''            '' |
| | Chinese dance, from ''Nutcracker Suite'' (Tchaikovsky) | C 2 | ''      ''            '' |

# A graded course of teaching material for the violin
## (Schools and methods of violin technic)

**First year**
| | |
|---|---|
| Graded lessons, Books 1, 2, and 3 | Louis J. Bostelmann |
| Fifty easy pieces, Book 1 | J. C. Kelley |
| Violin method, Book 1 | Hohmann-Bostelmann |
| Fundamental scale book | L. J. Bostelmann |

**Second year**
| | |
|---|---|
| Violin method, Book 2 | Hohmann-Bostelmann |
| Etudes, Op. 20, Book 1 | Kayser |
| Violin method, Book 2 | Laoureaux |
| Etudes, Op. 45, Book 1 | Wohlfahrt |

**Third year**
| | |
|---|---|
| Fundamental scales, Book 2 | L. J. Bostelmann |
| Violin method, Book 3 | Hohmann-Bostelmann |
| School of violin technic Op. 1, Book 2 | Sevčik |
| Etudes, Op. 45, Book 2 | Wohlfahrt |

**Fourth year**
| | |
|---|---|
| Progressive studies, Book 1; first, second and third positions | Gruenberg |
| Etudes, Op. 20, Books 2 and 3 | Kayser |
| School of violin technic, Op 1, Book 3 | Sevčik |

**Fifth year**
| | |
|---|---|
| Progressive studies, Book 2; fourth, fifth, sixth and seventh positions | Gruenberg |
| Forty-two etudes, from No. 2 to No. 26 | Kreutzer |
| Etudes, Op. 36, Book 2 | Mazas |
| School of violin technic, Op. 1, Book 4 | Sevčik |

**Sixth year**
| | |
|---|---|
| Thirty-six caprices (selected) | Fiorillo |
| Forty-two etudes, from No. 27 to No. 42 | Kreutzer |
| School of violin technic, Op. 1, Books 2 and 3 | Sevčik |

**Seventh year**
| | |
|---|---|
| Studies, Op. 35, twenty-four etudes | Dont |
| Scale studies | Flesch |
| Twenty-four studies (matinées) | Gaviniés |
| Twenty-four études (caprices | Rode |
| Etude caprices, Op. 18 | Wieniawski |

**Eighth year**
| | |
|---|---|
| Sixty études-Ecole transcendante | De Beriot |
| Twenty-four caprices | Rode |
| Etudes, Op. 48 | Vieuxtemps |

**Ninth year**
| | |
|---|---|
| Caprices, Op. 1 | Paganini |
| Etudes, Ecole moderne | Wieniawski |

# VIOLA AND PIANO, OR VIOLA ALONE

| COMPOSER | TITLE, KEY & OP. | GR. | REMARKS |
|---|---|---|---|
| Aguirre, Julián | Huella (Heifetz) | C 2 | Movido y energico, also declamatory, playful and singing. |
| Bach, Carl Ph. Em. | Concerto in D Major for Violin, (transscribed for viola by H. Casadesus) | C 2 | Allegro moderato ♩ = 88, festive and jubilant.<br><br>Andante, lento molto ♪ = 88, affectionate and expressive.<br><br>Allegretto ♩.= 76, gay and lively. |
| Bach, Johann Sebastian | Six suites originally written for violoncello solo, adapted for the viola by Louis Svečenski | C 1 | Suite No. 1<br><br>Allegro moderato (quasi andante) ♩ = 70, imaginative and at times quite rubato.<br><br>Allamande, molto moderato ♩ = 63, eloquent and expressive; inviting to rubato playing.<br><br>Courante (Allegro non troppo) ♩ = 96, gay and joyful; at times tender and expressive.<br><br>Sarabande (Lento) ♪ = 86, warm and affectionate.<br><br>Menuetto 1 (Moderato) ♩ = 100, stately and dignified.<br><br>Menuetto 2 ♩ = 108, graceful and distinguished.<br><br>Gigue (Allegro vivo) ♩ = 108, spirited and gay.<br><br>Suite No. 2<br><br>Prelude (Allegro moderato) ♩ = 69, eloquent and warm; inviting to rubato playing. |

| COMPOSER | TITLE, KEY & OP. | GR. | REMARKS |
|---|---|---|---|
| Bach, Johann Sebastian (Cont.) | Six suites originally written for violon-cello solo, adapted for the viola by Louis Svečenski (Cont.) | C 1 | Suite No. 2 (Cont.) |

Allemande (Molto moderato) ♪ = 48, expressive, imaginative and dignified.

Courante (Allegro non troppo) ♩ = 84, refreshing, sweeping and flowing.

Sarabande (Lento) ♪ = 86, affectionate and singing.

Menuetto 1 (Moderato) ♩ = 104, stately.

Menuetto 2 ♩ = 104, graceful.

Gigue (Vivace) ♪. = 72, gay and lively.

### Suite No. 3

Prelude (Allegro) ♩ = 74-78, eloquent, free and imaginative.

Allemande ♩ = 66, stately but with sweep.

Courante ♩ = 132, spirited and lively.

Sarabande ♪ = 80, affectionate and singing.

Bourrée 1 ♩ = 80, gay and sprightly.

Bourrée 2 ♩ = 74, expressive and singing.

Gigue ♪. = 84, gay and lively.

### Suite No. 4

Prelude ♩ = 120, dignified.

Allemande ♩ = 80, eloquent but flowing.

Corrente ♩ = 100, joyful, at times affectionate.

| Bach, Johann Sebastian (Cont.) | Six suites originally written for violoncello solo, adapted for the viola by Louis Svečenski (Cont.) | C 1 | Suite No. 4 (Cont.) |

Sarabande ♪ = 92, expressive and tender.

Loure 1 ♩ = 104, easy flowing and graceful.

Loure 2 ♩ = 104, kind and friendly.

Gigue ♩. = 112, spirited and with sweep.

Suite No. 5

Prelude (Adagio) ♪ = 84, eloquent expressive and free.

Allegro moderato ♩. = 80, spirited and lively.

Allemande ♩ = 66-69, stately and eloquent.

Corrente ♩ = 66, easy flowing.

Sarabande ♩ = 70, warm and with great fervor.

Gavotte 1 ♩ = 82, gay and lively.

Gavotte 2 ♩ = 82, easy flowing but with sweep.

Gigue ♩ = 76, spirited and gay; at times expressive.

Suite No. 6

Prelude ♩. = 104-108, dashing and with great sweep.

Allemande ♪ = 48, eloquent, warm and affectionate.

Corrente ♩ = 123, happy and spirited.

Sarabande ♩ = 50, kind and affectionate.

| COMPOSER | TITLE, KEY & OP. | GR. | REMARKS |
|---|---|---|---|
| Bach, Johann Sebastian (Cont.) | Six suites originally written for violoncello solo, adapted for the viola by Louis Svečenski (Cont.) | C 1 | Suite 6 (Cont.)<br><br>Gavotte 1 ♩ = 86, gay and lively.<br><br>Gavotte 2 ♩ = 86, graceful and friendly.<br><br>Gigue ♩.= 94, spirited, festive and joyful. |
| | Adagio, from the Organ Concerto No. 3 (after Vivaldi) (transcribed for viola by V. Borissovsky) | C 2 | Eloquent, expressive and flexible, like a recitativo. |
| | Adagio, from the Toccata in C Major for Organ, (transcribed by A. Siloti;) viola part revised by L. Tertis | C 2 | Fervent, affectionate and eloquent; also at times serene. |
| Benjamin, Arthur | Jamaica Rumba (arr. for viola by W. Primrose) | C 2 | Tempo giusto-alla rumba, gay and jazzy. |
| Bloch, Ernest | Suite for viola and piano | C 3 | Lento ♪ = 84-92, mysterious; at times dramatic and passionate. The meno lento ♩ = 60 is doleful and expressive, building up to great fervor. The allegro ♩ = 120-132 is joyful and gay, at times exalted and singing. The largamente ♩ = 69 is eloquent and broad but changes to spiritual transfiguration.<br><br>Allegro ironico ♩ = 120, spirited and very rhythmical. The grave (moderato) ♩ = 58 is mysterious and also expressive.<br><br>Lento ♩ = 50, poetic and expressive; at times eloquent.<br><br>Molto vivo ♩ = 152, joyful and gay. The moderato assai ♩ = 80 is lofty and<br>(Cont.) |

| COMPOSER | TITLE, KEY & OP. | GR. | REMARKS |
|---|---|---|---|
| Bloch, Ernest (Cont.) | Suite for viola and piano (Cont.) | C 3 | eloquent. The animato (non troppo) ♩ = 144-152 is playful. The presto is restless and excited. The largamente ♩ = 66, is eloquent; it has moments of sublimity. The molto vivo ♩ = 160 brings the movement to a climactic close. |
| Brahms, Johannes | Waltz, Op. 39, No. 15 (transcribed for viola from A major to D major by V. Borissovsky) | C 3 | Moderato, tender and affectionate; double-stops throughout. |
| | Sonata in F Minor, Op. 120, No. 1 | C 3 | Allegro appassionato ♩ = 120, serious and eloquent, affectionate and warm. There are sections of great rhythmical vitality. The coda strikes a tragic note, but ends in sublime transfiguration.<br><br>Andante un poco adagio ♪ = 70, serene, in a way spiritual; yet warm and affectionate.<br><br>Allegro grazioso ♩ = 144, graceful, friendly and affectionate; also at times joyful. The middle section is warm and singing.<br><br>Vivace ♩ = 96, joyful and manly; also graceful, caressing and playful. The semplice theme is tender and friendly. The movement closes in a mood of exaltation and jubilation. |
| | Sonata in E-flat Major, Op. 120, No. 2 | C 3 | Allegro amabile ♩ = 100. The opening is friendly and affectionate; building up to intense fervor and enthusiasm. The sotto voce is tender and caressing. The entire movement conveys a mood of springtime; of hope and optimism. |

| COMPOSER | TITLE, KEY & OP. | GR. | REMARKS |
|---|---|---|---|
| Brahms, Johannes (Cont.) | Sonata in E-flat Major, Op. 120, No. 2 (Cont.) | C 3 | Appassionata ma non troppo allegro ♩ = 144, rich and full; at times tenderly wooing. The sostenuto ♩ = 120 is warm and singing. |
| | | | Andante con moto ♪ = 114, friendly and sunny; at times playful. |
| | | | Allegro non troppo ♩ = 112, joyful and enthusiastic, the più tranquillo ♩ = 84 is warm and affectionate. In the last eighteen bars a return of the allegro non troppo tempo seems indicated, to end the movement in a mood of joy and triumph. |
| Caix Hervelois, Paul de | Mélancolie d'amour (R. Frost) | B 3 | Moderato, quietly singing. |
| Chopin, Frédéric | Nocturne in C-sharp Minor, (posthumous) (Vardi) | C 2 | Lento con espressione, poetic, tender and affectionate. |
| Clarke, Rebecca | Passacaglia on an old English tune | C 1 | Grave, ma non troppo lento, serious and dignified. |
| Corelli, Arcangelo | Cello Sonata in D Minor (transcribed for viola by Milton Katims) | C 1 | Largo ♩ = 68, eloquent. |
| | | | Allemande (Allegro) ♩ = 112, spirited and gay. |
| | | | Sarabande (Largo) ♩ = 56, affectionate and quietly singing. |
| | | | Giga (Allegro) ♩ = 96, spirited and with sweep; at times playful. |
| Enesco, Georges | Concert piece | C 3 | An important concert number. Eloquent, warmhearted and romantic; often brilliant. |
| Fauré, Gabriel | Lamento | C 1 | Andante, doleful and expressive. |
| Frost, Rudolph | Homage to Ravel | B 3 | Andantino ♪ = 69, poetic and imaginative. |

| COMPOSER | TITLE, KEY & OP. | GR. | REMARKS |
|---|---|---|---|
| Giorni, Aurelio | Sonata in D Minor for Cello and Piano (with alternate part for viola) | C 3 | Allegro con fuoco ♩= 138, suggesting great sweep and drive. |
| | | | Allegretto, easy flowing and graceful. |
| | | | Scherzo, witty, spirited and graceful. |
| | | | Adagio, stately and majestic. |
| | | | Allegro vivace, joyful. |
| Glazunov, Alexander | Elegy, Op. 44 | C 1 | Allegretto ♩.= 72, easy flowing, singing and graceful; also somewhat wistful. |
| Goldmark, Karl | Veil dance, from ''Queen of Sheba'' (transcribed by (R. Frost) | C 2 | Allegro moderato, singing and suave. |
| Granados, Enrique | Orientale (Spanish Dance No. 2) (Milton Katims) | B 3 | Andante, wistful and tender; use of harmonics. |
| Handel, George F. | Cello Sonata in G Minor (transcribed for viola by (Milton Katims) | C 1 | Grave ♪= 58, majestic and dignified. |
| | | | Allegro ♩ = 112, spirited and lively. |
| | | | Sarabande (Largo) ♩= 58, singing and affectionate. |
| | | | Allegro ♩ = 104-106, spirited, and with rhythmical vitality. |
| Harris, Roy | Soliloquy and dance for viola and piano | C 3 | Soliloquy. The opening is wistful and introspect, building up to intense fervor; ending in a retrospect mood. |
| | | | Dance, gay and joyful. |
| Haydn, Franz Joseph | Cello Concerto in D Major, (transcribed for viola by A. Spitzner) | C 3 | Allegro moderato ♩= 63, sunny and affectionate. |
| | | | Adagio ♪= 69, warm and singing. |
| | | | Allegro ♩.= 96, happy and playful. |

| COMPOSER | TITLE, KEY & OP. | GR. | REMARKS |
|---|---|---|---|
| Hindemith, Paul | Sonata for viola and piano, Op. 11, No. 4 | C 3 | A forceful and vital piece. <u>Fantasie</u>, the opening is quiet and persuasive, building up to great eloquence. The movement gives the impression of an improvisation. |
| | | | <u>Theme with Variations,</u> the theme is a simple folksong. The variations develop great contrasts in mood and character, building up in the coda of the finale to a wild and exciting climax. |
| d'Indy, Vincent | Lied, Op. 19 | C 1 | <u>Andantino</u> <u>non</u> <u>troppo,</u> easy flowing and quietly singing. The <u>plus aminé</u> is somewhat more flowing. |
| Jacobi, Frederick | Fantasy for viola and piano | C 3 | A dramatic work, rhapsodic in character. |
| Kalinnikov, Basil | Chanson Triste | B 3 | A short piece in 5/4 time; sustained and wistful in character. |
| Leclair, Jean Marie | Sonata, from ''Le Tombeau'' | C 3 | <u>Grave</u> ♪ = 58, serious and eloquent. <br><br> <u>Allegro</u> ma non troppo ♩ = 69, playful and easy flowing. <br><br> <u>Gavotte</u> (<u>Allegro</u> <u>grazioso</u>) ♩ = 54-58, light and graceful. <br><br> <u>Allegro</u> ♩. = 76, gay and spirited. |
| Marais, Marin | Five old dances for viola with pianoforte accompaniment, (M. E. Aldis and L. T. Rowe) | B 3 | 1. <u>L'agréable</u> (<u>Rondo</u>) (<u>Moderato</u>) ♪ = 78, sunny and friendly. <br><br> 2. <u>La Provençale</u> (<u>Gai</u>) ♪ =84, light and happy. <br><br> 3. <u>La Musette</u>(<u>Moderato</u>) ♩ = 66, comfortable and graceful. |

| COMPOSER | TITLE, KEY & OP. | GR. | REMARKS |
|---|---|---|---|
| Marais, Marin (Cont.) | Five old dances for viola with pianoforte accompaniment, (M. E. Aldis and L. T. Rowe) (Cont.) | | 4. La Matelotte(Gaiement) ♪ = 118, gay and lively.<br><br>5. Le Basque (Vivace) ♩ = 138, spirited and lively. |
| Marcello, Benedetto | Sonata in F Major (Vardi) | C 1 | Largo ♪ = 69, dignified and eloquent, but also affection-ate.<br><br>Allegro ♩ = 116, spirited and gay.<br><br>Largo ♩ = 74, serious and dignified.<br><br>Presto ♩ = 132, light and lively. |
| | Sonata in G Major (A. Gibson) | B 3 | Andante ♪ = 68, friendly, and with simplicity.<br><br>Allegro ♩ = 116, spirited and gay.<br><br>Grave ♩ = 74, noble and dignified.<br><br>Allegro ♩. = 78, light and playful. |
| Mozart, Wolfgang A. | Clarinette Concerto in A Major (Köchel No. 622) (transcribed for viola) | C 3 | Allegro ♩ = 126, sunny and and happy.<br><br>Adagio ♩ = 60, poetic and tenderly singing.<br><br>Rondo (allegro) ♩. = 89, spirited, lively and gay. |
| Mussorgsky, Modest P. | Hopak (Ukrainian dance) (transcribed by V. Borissovsky) | C 2 | Allegretto Scherzando, gay and lively; featuring double-stops, left-hand pizzicato, harmonics, and spiccato. |
| Purcell, Henry | Aria (transcribed by Milton Katims) | C 1 | Lento espressivo, noble and affectionate. |
| Ravel, Maurice | Pavane for viola and harp (or piano) | C 1 | Tender and expressive. |
| Schubert, Franz | Sonata in A Minor ("Arpeggione") (transcribed for viola | C 3 | Allegro moderato ♩ = 112, tender and affectionate; also playful and witty. |

| COMPOSER | TITLE, KEY & OP. | GR. | REMARKS |
|---|---|---|---|
| Schubert, Franz (Cont.) | and piano by Milton Katims) | | Adagio ♩ = 68, tenderly singing, but with great simplicity. |
| | | | Allegretto ♩ = 126, easy flowing and friendly; at times playful and sparkling. |
| Schumann, Robert | Pictures from Fairy Land, Op. 113 | C 1 | 1. Nicht schnell (Moderato) ♩ = 88, affectionate and singing. |
| | | C 1 | 2. Lebhaft (Vivace) ♪ = 104-108, exuberant and joyful. |
| | | | 3. Rasch (Vivace) ♩ = 97, agitated and restless. |
| | | | 4. Langsam mit melancholischem Ausdruck ♪ = 69, wistful and tenderly singing. |
| Senaillé, Jean Baptiste | Allegro spirituoso | C 1 | Très vite ♩ = 138, a short, spirited and lively piece; featuring spiccato and ricochet bowing. |
| Stamitz, Karl | Concerto in D Major, Op. 1 | C 3 | Allegro ♩ = 120, spirited and joyful. |
| | | | Andante moderato ♪ = 70-72, affectionate and tender. |
| | | | Rondo ♩ = 132, gay, lively and playful. |
| Vaughan Williams, Ralph | Suite for viola and orchestra (pianoforte) | C 2 | Group 1 |
| | | | No. 1, Prelude (Allegro moderato) ♪ = 66, dignified and serious. |
| | | | No. 2, Carol (Andante con moto) ♪ = 70, unassuming and singing. |
| | | | No. 3, Christmas dance (Allegro) ♪° = 66, happy and and gay; featuring playful change in rhythm. |

| COMPOSER | TITLE, KEY & OP. | GR. | REMARKS |
|---|---|---|---|
| Vaughan Williams, Ralph (Cont.) | Suite for viola and orchestra (Pianoforte) (Cont.) | C 2 | **Group 2**<br><br>No. 1, Ballad (Lento non troppo) ♩ = 54, tenderly singing.<br><br>No. 2, Moto perpetuo (Allegro) ♩ = 80, featuring interesting play of rhythm in fast 16th passages throughout.<br><br>**Group 3**<br><br>No. 1, Musette (Lento) ♩ = 58, softly singing (with sordino).<br><br>No. 2 Polka melancholique (Molto moderato) ♩ = 72,<br><br>No. 3, Galop (Allegro molto) ♩ = 166, lively and spirited. |
| Veracini, F. M. | Largo (M. Katims) | B 3 | A short and slow piece; affectionate and very expressive. |
| Vitali, Tommaso | Ciacona (L. Bailly) | C 3 | Molto moderato ♩ = 69, theme and variations of a serious and dignified character, bringing into use many different types of bowing. |
| Vitetta, Marius | Etude Caprice No. 1 in E Minor | C 3 | Allegro con brio, spirited and lively; featuring double-stops, trills, spiccato and staccato bowings. Also fingered octaves. A difficult and brilliant short piece. |
| Vivaldi, Antonio | Intermezzo, from Concerto Grosso in D Minor (Sam Franko) | B 3 | Andantino cantabile ♩ = 100, affectionate and singing; also graceful and easy flowing. |

# TECHNICAL STUDY MATERIAL FOR THE VIOLA

Bruni.  Twenty-five melodious studies.

Campagnoli.  Forty-one caprices.

Dolejsi.  Modern viola technique.

Dont, J.  Op. 35:  Twenty-four viola studies.

Dont, J.  Twenty progressive studies.

Flesch, C.  Scale studies.

Gifford, A. M.  Twenty studies for viola.

Hermann, F.  Op. 18:  Six concert studies.

Kreutzer.  Forty-two études.

Kreuz.  Op. 40:  Progressive studies (four books).

Kreuz.  Select studies  (four books).

Lifschey.  Daily technical studies.

Lifschey.  Scales and arpeggios (two books).

Lifschey.  Twelve modulatory studies (Campagnoli).

Rode.  Twenty-four caprices.

Sevčik.  Op. 1:  Books 1 and 2.


Note:

Since most viola students start their musical training as violinists, I have gathered study material of an advanced grade only, assuming that they have had the necessary technical foundation as violinists when they change over from the violin to the viola.

Date Loaned

Demco 292-5